Climb

Cyclist Climb

The most epic cycling ascents in the world

MITCHELL BEAZLEY

Contents

Chapter 4:

France 106

Chapter 5:

The Rest of the World 190

Introduction

Defining a classic climb isn't easy. Some ascents have the weight of numbers behind them: monstrous gradients and eye-watering elevation. Others have history, and the echoes of great battles fought by the legends of bicycle racing on their roads. For some it might be their natural beauty; others are feats of engineering. Yet all of them are united by one crucial aspect: the challenge of conquering them by bike, a challenge that can immerse a cyclist in suffering along the way, but with the promise of euphoria at the summit.

Cyclist magazine has spent its existence exploring these climbs, and here we have picked 35 of the very best, each one ridden from foot to summit with ride statistics logged and stunning photography captured. The big question is: where to start?

There are the great European mountain ranges, where so many summits have been made famous by the Grand Tours of France, Italy and Spain, with names that will send a shiver down the spines of pro and amateur cyclists alike: Alpe d'Huez, Col du Tourmalet, Passo dello Stelvio, Mortirolo and Alto de l'Angliru to name just a few. There are also climbs that seem to exist purely for their own sake, such as the stunning Sa Calobra in Mallorca or Trollstigen in Norway. Other climbs aren't quite so long and steep but do present their own challenges, such as the cobbled Mur de Huy or Muur van Geraardsbergen in Belgium. Others are even longer and steeper, for example the monster Mauna Kea in Hawaii and Pikes Peak in Colorado, USA.

The choice is yours, but wherever you start you can be sure of an epic adventure along the way.

Oh, and there is one final point to consider. Given that each of these 35 climbs ends at a summit, that means there are 35 descents for you to enjoy as well. See you at the bottom.

Italy

Summit height: 2,340m *(7,677ft)*
Altitude gain: 568m *(1,863ft)*
Length: 7.5km *(4½ miles)*
Average gradient: 7.5%
Maximum gradient: 18%

Tre Cime di Lavaredo

Winding through the limestone spires of the Italian Dolomites, this climb is as fierce as it is beautiful.

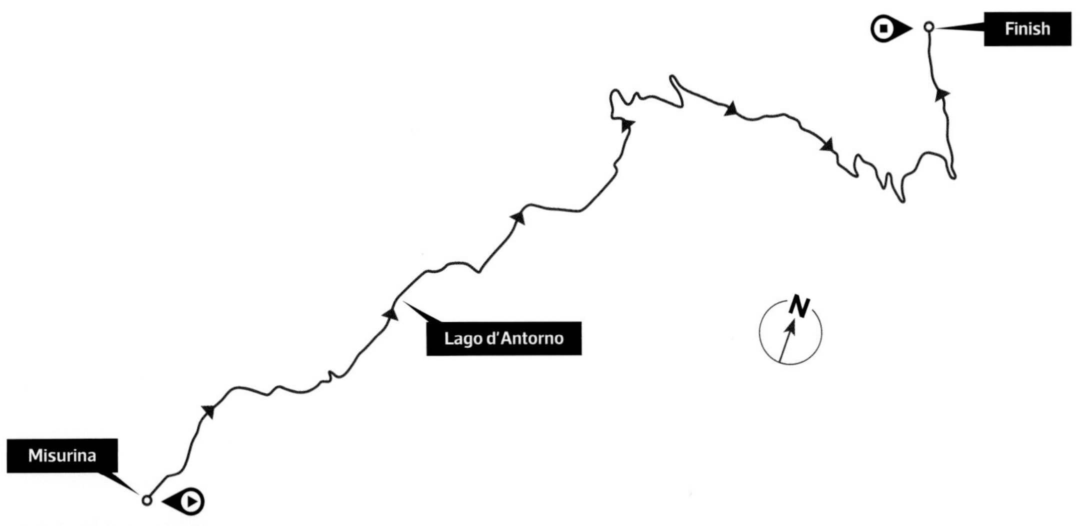

Length. Average gradient. Maximum gradient. Summit height. Figures that frame a climb. In some ways they seem to tell you so much, but in reality they tell you so little.

Standing in northern Italy, surrounded by the pale limestone peaks of the Sexten Dolomites, the task that lies ahead, if expressed in those terms, is as follows: 7.5km (4½ miles), averaging 7.5%, maxing out at 18%, and finishing at 2,340m (7,677ft). On paper, then, the climb of the Tre Cime di Lavaredo (or Drei Zinnen, in German – for this marks the linguistic boundary between the Italian-speaking Veneto and the predominantly German-speaking South Tyrol that was part of Austria until 1919) sounds bearable. Not too long, not too steep and not too high at the finish.

Mentally translate those figures into the toll that you will feel in your legs and you would probably label it as about average – in fact, the figures are so unexceptional that you might even ignore this dead-end climb when planning a cycling holiday in the region. However, for so many reasons, it would be a mistake to underestimate Tre Cime.

Very early or later in the day are the best times to tackle the climb, because you'll either beat the crowds or let them subside. We're not talking vast pelotons >>

>> of riders, either, but crowds of cars and coaches. By 10am in high season, the two large car parks at the bottom will be packed and plenty more will pay the toll to reach the road that lies beyond a striped red and white barrier. If you have time to kill, you could wait in a bar in the small settlement of Misurina at the bottom of the climb – the pizzas are excellent.

When you do clip in, you'll find a tough start. The road is well surfaced, but winds through hairpins for an opening stretch that averages 11% – considerably more than the advertised 7.5%. Like the prologue at the beginning of a Shakespeare play, it's a shortened foretelling of the main acts still to come.

Next up is that harbinger of softened gradients – a lake. Entirely natural and not very large, it lies still, reflecting the trees in its mirror surface. Things get easier still as the road descends through a switchback to the toll collectors, where cars must pay their dues.

Carry speed off the descent and hold it along another flat section that winds across a small bridge. It's all very pleasant, but if you look up you will see the Refugio Auronzo that you're aiming for. Although it's getting closer, the altitude difference between you and it isn't really decreasing, and that's a worry.

Just 4km (2½ miles) of the climb remains by this point, but there's still around 500m (1,640ft) of climbing to be done – not much less than there was at the start. That 7.5% average is now looking horribly deceptive. Try more like 12%.

With the next right-hand hairpin you start to climb once more and this time it won't let up until the finish. The fir trees that line the road stay with you for another couple of kilometres, only occasionally parting to offer a narrow view on a hairpin. Then, on a switchback with some red graffiti reminding you where you are, you emerge to be treated to the full IMAX experience. If your breath isn't short enough already, there's a good chance it will be taken away entirely by the sheer grandeur of the landscape.

From here, the road twists back and forth on itself for a kilometre, and as much as you might want to stare at your surroundings you're now into perhaps the toughest segment of the whole climb, as it ramps up, then eases, then ramps up again. It may only be a short climb, but that's why it can explode a race and time gaps can be surprisingly large at the summit.

Look back at video footage of Stage 15 of the 2007 Giro d'Italia, where the infamous Riccardo Riccò pipped his Saunier Duval teammate, Leonardo Piepoli, to the summit, and you can see the carnage that these slopes unleash on the riders as they battle upwards. Their shoulders are rocking and rolling, and mouths are hanging wide open. Danilo Di Luca in the pink jersey behind them wasn't faring any better.

Look back further in time and even the grainy footage of 1968 can't disguise the effort wracking the body of >>

On a switchback with some red graffiti, you emerge to the full IMAX experience

P
riservato

>> Eddy Merckx as he pounds his way to the top. It's as though the climb is designed to sap the finesse from the pedal strokes of even the most graceful of cyclists.

The other thing that seems to categorize this climb is the often inclement weather. Surely one of the most famous images from recent Grand Tours must be Vincenzo Nibali crossing the line in the snow in Stage 20 of the Giro in 2013.

Thankfully, the sun does shine on Tre Cime di Lavaredo sometimes, and when it does the scenery is simply stunning. It has the sublime air of a climb that has been wrought in a digital fantasy like Zwift and then brought to life. Even the cowbells seem more musical.

As you round the last left-hand hairpin, you're faced with a straight run to the end, but any thoughts of a sprint finish are quelled by the fact that the gradient now hangs between 13% and 14%. If you can afford the energy to look over the edge of the road to your left, you will see the switchbacks, and beyond that the lake among the trees below. It has the appearance of a model landscape.

At the very top, your reward is the most incredible viewing platform. With the *tre cime* themselves (three peaks: Piccola, Grande and Ovest – Little, Big and Western) behind you, it's quite the panorama. The German word *zinnen* means the upright part of a battlement on a castle wall and it's a perfect description of the peaks that seem to form a natural fortress around you. The Dolomites might not be the highest mountains in Europe, but like the climb to get here they offer a view to which bare facts can't possibly do justice.

2400
2200
2000
1800
1600m
0km 1 2 3 4 5 6 7 7.5

Monte Grappa

In the foothills of the Italian Dolomites, Monte Grappa is a giant climb with a history of battles on the bike and bloodshed during the two World Wars.

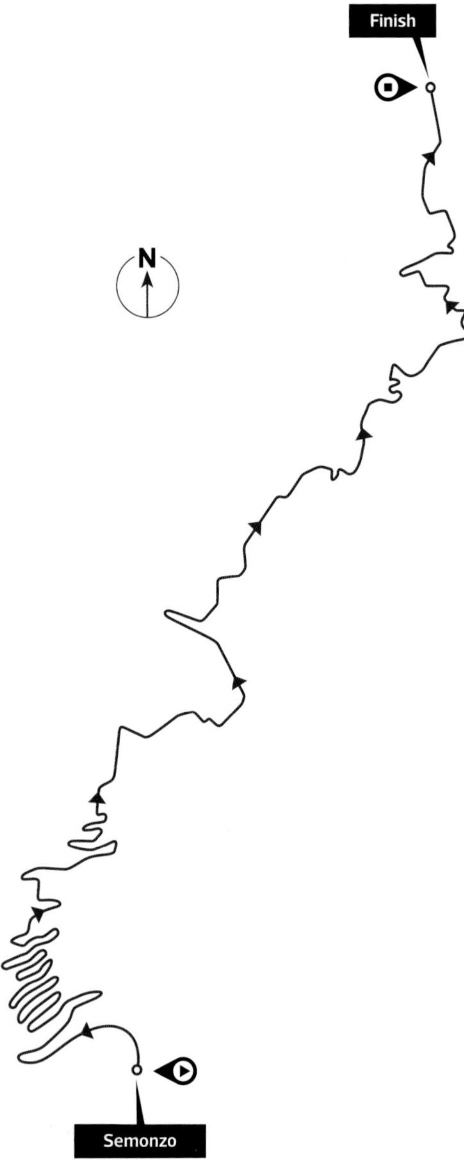

Make sure you give yourself time to pause at the top of Monte Grappa. Once you've got your breath back, go for a walk. The temptation might be to throw yourself into the descent before your muscles get cold, but don't. Instead, follow the steps out of the car park and climb up a little further to the summit proper. Why? Because this mountain and its history are much, much bigger than cycling.

That's not to belittle the exploits of Merckx, Quintana, et al., but it would be inappropriate to talk about their suffering on these slopes given the scenes of conflict that this mountain has witnessed.

Three major battles were fought here towards the end of the First World War and it was Italy's resistance on the slopes of Monte Grappa that stopped the rampant Austrian army from sweeping down through the country. Huge losses were suffered on both sides, and it's well worth remembering this as you climb the slopes. Let your tyres tread lightly.

Monte Grappa offers an array of different ways up its vast slopes, but the one we chose is from Semonzo. It runs from the southern side and neighbours the 'classic' route from Romano d'Ezzelino. However, at 19km (12 miles) long, this route is about 7km ($4\frac{1}{3}$ miles) shorter and therefore much steeper, averaging 8.1% to the classic's 5.9%. It's also the route used on Stage 14 of the 2010 Giro d'Italia (won by Vincenzo Nibali) and the 2014 Giro's Stage 19 mountain time-trial, won by Nairo Qj21uintana, who took just 1hr 5min 37sec to reach the top from the centre of town.

The climb begins by a church with the miniaturized architecture of a cathedral that has been in a hot wash. Next to it is a memorial to members of the Italian resistance in the two World Wars, a landmark that will gain greater significance by the summit.

Set off into the trees on the lower slopes and you're straight into a regimented concentration of hairpins >>

>> with 16 switchbacks crammed into about 6km (3¾ miles). On the westerly hairpins, the trees often recede, offering up views back across Semonzo and the Venetian Plain beyond.

Such is the steepness of the slope that by the first hairpin it feels as if you're looking down from a hot air balloon. A couple of hairpins later, you're viewing the tiny buildings from a light aircraft.

After about 7km (4⅓ miles) you emerge from the trees to some scattered houses, but you're not out of the woods yet. As you plunge back into the dense deciduous tunnel, you'll find that the gradient eases and even reverses briefly, letting your legs recover slightly as you shoot through an arch of rock. Make the most of it, though, as it is a precursor to the hardest section of the climb, with 2km (1¼ miles) at more than 10%.

The trees gradually recede to your right as you climb the narrow but well-surfaced road, revealing attractive rolling pastures. Hairpin number 22 is a welcome sight, as it means you're nearly at the end of the hardest section. A couple of hundred metres later you reach a crest and see the top of the mountain for the first time. It's still 5km (3 miles) away, but it's nice to have a target.

A brief plunge downhill through a couple of very fast, sweeping corners is so enjoyable that you'll almost want to turn round and climb back up so that you can do them again, but you're now in a beautiful little green bowl that you must climb out of before continuing on to the summit.

These more open upper slopes in the final kilometres afford wonderful views, and although the road feels remote there is a surprisingly manicured air to the mountain.

Soon, the routes from Colmirano and Pederobba join the road, like tributaries flowing uphill into a tarmac river. Then, as you reach a steep junction where you turn right, you might catch sight of a bronze sculpture by Augusto Murer down the slope.

During the Second World War, the anti-fascist partisans from this area took Monte Grappa as their base in 1943, after the fall of Mussolini, but Nazi forces crushed them in 1944, either killing them in a brutal rout on the mountain or hanging them afterwards. The sculpture is a memorial to those partisans, including those mentioned on the memorial at the bottom of the climb.

The Giro d'Italia rarely heads all the way to the summit, usually preferring to pass along the ridge road just below the top without venturing onto the dead-end road to the 1,775m (5,823ft) peak. That final stretch is a nasty end for tired legs, rearing up for one final time to over 12%. If it's cold, you can warm up in the cafe at the top, but afterwards you should take that walk out of the car park, up the steps.

It leads to a huge, white stone structure, tiered like a compressed wedding cake. Finding something of this scale on top of a mountain is deeply impressive. It is not just a memorial to those who died on the

mountain during the First World War, but an ossuary. Bronze plaques denote the resting places of those whose bodies were identified. A famous one reads 'Peter Pan' – the association with the boy who never grew up being heartbreakingly fitting.

All told, the bones of 22,910 Italian and Austro-Hungarian soldiers lie here, fewer than 3,000 of them with a name attached. To put that in context, Tyne Cot, the largest Commonwealth cemetery in Flanders and indeed the world, holds 11,965 bodies.

It is sobering and yet the view is also spectacular. You can see the winding roads on the slopes below you and they are beautiful, but you don't need a background in military tactics to also instantly appreciate why this mountain was so strategically important during the World Wars.

Some climbs stick in your memory for the aches the ascent imparts to your legs. Others remain memorable because of the views they offer up as you pedal. Some feel special because they're scenes of fabled Grand Tour showdowns. And some, however much you love the sport, transcend anything to do with cycling. Monte Grappa is one such place.

Mortirolo

With a name to strike fear into the hearts of even pro cyclists, the Mortirolo is a favourite test piece of the Giro d'Italia.

You have to be a cyclist to understand the appeal of the Mortirolo. It's too narrow and poorly surfaced to be fun in a car or on a motorbike, and the main road provides a faster and easier route between Mazzo and Monno. Unlike the nearby Stelvio and Gavia, there are no real views to stand and gaze over. No Michelin-starred cuisine or site of special scientific interest awaits you on the summit either. A compulsion to don Lycra and pedal is therefore imperative if you're to be inspired by these slopes. Take anyone else over the Mortirolo and they will have forgotten all about it as soon as they finish descending it.

Even the world of cycling wasn't aware of the Passo del Mortirolo (also known as the Passo della Foppa) until relatively recently, and what's more it almost robbed us of one of the Giro's most famous stages. In 1988, the Gavia was still stacked with spring snow and the authorities were wondering if it might be a bit too chilly for the riders. The nearby Mortirolo, which summits nearly 1,000m (3,281ft) lower than >>

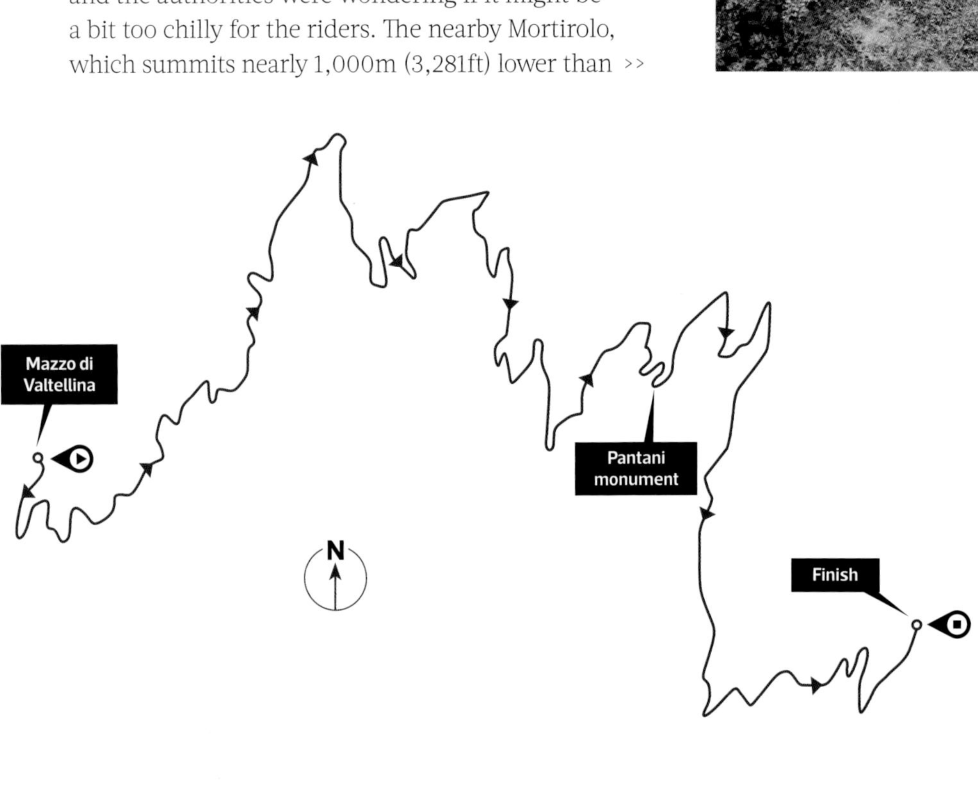

Summit height: 1,852m ***(6,076ft)***
Altitude gain: 1,251m ***(4,104ft)***
Length: 11.86km ***($7^{1}/_{3}$ miles)***
Average gradient: 11%
Maximum gradient: 20%

>> the Gavia, was suggested as an alternative. The commissaires decided a little bit of frostbite wouldn't do the peloton too much harm and as a result we have the images of Andy Hampsten battling valiantly through the snow.

Although it wasn't used in 1988, the Mortirolo's presence had been noted, and in 1990 it made its Giro d'Italia debut. That first year, the riders ascended from Monno, but the steep descent was deemed too treacherous in hindsight, so in 1991 the route went in the opposite direction and the rest is history.

On the way to the Mortirolo, it seems natural to ride through the sleepy streets of Mazzo di Valtellina first, admiring the Alpine architecture and cream-coloured walls that lie in the valley between the wooded slopes. However, it's almost impossible to avoid juddering across some cobbles if you cycle through the centre of town, and that might not be the preparation your body needs.

Follow the small brown signs south towards Salita del Mortirolo (climb of the Mortirolo) and after a few twists and turns you'll see the large, craggy piece of pale rock that marks the official start of the climb on Via Valle. The climb is narrow from the start and the first few hairpins snake through orchards. The next point of interest is the imposing, if slightly dishevelled, Castello di Pedenale, which sits on a prominent hillock next to the road. It was built by the powerful Venosta family in the 12th century and was part of a network of defences around the Mortirolo Pass.

Bar a church and one notable monument that we'll get to in a bit, that's really it for sights. Past the castle you plunge into the mainly deciduous trees that are densely spread across the mountain, and most of the climb is spent beneath branches. If it's sunny, you'll be glad of the shade, even while cursing the slightly stifling nature of the still air. And you'll definitely notice the nature of the air, because you'll be sucking in great lungfuls of the stuff.

Between kilometres three and six ($1^3/_4$–$3^3/_4$ miles), right in the heart of this 12-km ($7^1/_2$-mile) ascent, the gradient averages between 11% and 14%. It's relentless. There's no other word for it.

It doesn't have the severe spikes of the Angliru or Zoncolan (although you may see very brief flashes of 20% on your bike computer), but it grinds you down with its sustained steepness. It's like a boxer that doesn't possess a knockout punch, so just keeps pummelling you with hefty body blows.

At hairpin 14, you briefly emerge from the trees into a meadow. It was here that Alberto Contador danced away from a pain-faced Fabio Aru in the 2015 Giro, >>

>> which is even more impressive when you consider that this unsheltered stretch also throws a headwind at you to exacerbate the gradient.

Haul yourself through the next couple of tightly stacked switchbacks and you'll pass a more permanent reminder of a cyclist: a sculpture of Marco Pantani, Il Pirata. Mounted high on a wall, the sculpture shows Pantani in his classic attacking climbing position with his hands on the drops. He's looking back over his left shoulder, no doubt assessing the damage wrought on those left behind.

In 1994, Pantani was in his second full season and started the Giro in support of Claudio Chiappucci. However, he won the mountainous Stage 14 and the next day, after crossing the Stelvio, he attacked at the bottom of the Mortirolo and won again. This catapulted him both into the limelight and into second overall, behind eventual winner Evgeni Berzin but ahead of the mighty Miguel Induráin, who had won the race in both 1992 and 1993.

From here, there is still a third of the climb to go. Each hairpin has a number, counting down from 33, and they're ticked off with reasonable regularity, helping to break up the climb into smaller chunks. Until you reach hairpin 8, that is. From here to number 7, it's a tortuous 1.5km (1 mile), and it seems to last an eternity as you plug away through the trees.

Thankfully, not long after this you emerge from between the trunks for the final time and into something akin to heathland. Once here, you're over the worst, and after the final hairpin the gradient even eases enough to allow a sprint for the line so that you can pretend you're Pantani for a few pedal strokes.

As you reach the finish of the climb, it's worth remembering that this was also the start of something. Such was the intrigue generated by this ascent that the Vuelta felt it needed to respond and find something harder still. So, to grab its own headlines, the peloton was tortured on the Angliru. Then, keen not to be outdone, the Giro organizers in turn retaliated by sending the riders zigzagging up the Zoncolan.

But for many, the Mortirolo and its savage slopes will remain the original and hardest climb of them all, an assertion made by Lance Armstrong after training there. The wider world might not see the appeal, but if you're a cyclist, the Mortirolo is a must.

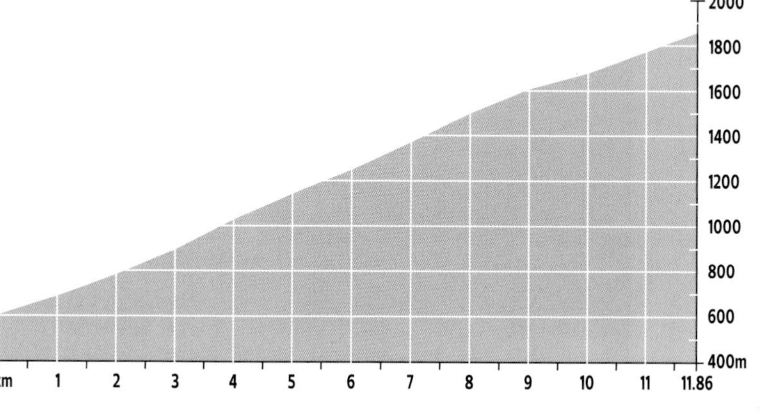

14

Summit height: 2,221m *(7,287ft)*
Altitude gain: 1,332m *(4,370ft)*
Length: 9.5km *(6 miles)*
Average gradient: 9%
Maximum gradient: 11%

Passo Giau

With its unrelenting gradient, 29 hairpins and disarming beauty, it's a wonder the Passo Giau doesn't have more of a Grand Tour heritage.

The Passo Giau is not a climb to start from the bottom. That's not to say you should start halfway up, but rather that you should start some way from the base of the climb near Selva di Cadore. Give yourself a run at it. Warm the legs, open up the lungs.

Most climbs take you straight into the gradient, rather like an intimidating first date: no preamble or drink at the bar, just, 'How many children do you envisage having and what's your salary?' >>

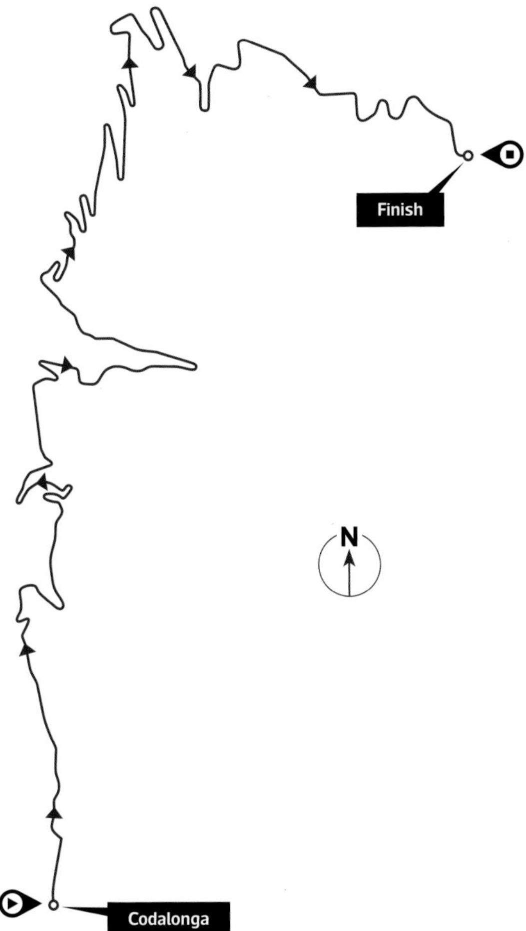

Unrelenting is probably the best description of this climb in the Dolomites

>> This approach can make things uncomfortable at first, but often the gradient will ease a little to let you recover and regroup. Sometimes, blissfully, the climb will even have a mild incline at the outset, perhaps wending a way through some meadows, such as on the Col d'Izoard. This allows a chance to spin freely before the hard work begins. If you're lucky, you even get some shade to shield you from the sun's glare as you ascend.

None of this applies to the Giau. Unrelenting is probably the best description of this 9.5-km (6-mile) climb in the Dolomites. And that's not unrelenting at a manageable 6% or 7%, but rather unrelenting between 9% and 11%. All right, there is a very brief dip to just below 8%, but that's not really a rest – it's more a case of finding a slightly smoother piece of wall to bang your head against. But there's a reason the harder southern side of the Giau is the more famous: its setting is just so distractingly beautiful.

The turning off the SP251 onto the SP638 feels like the natural start to the climb, and instantly it's picture-postcard stuff. The Codalonga river runs next to and sometimes underneath the road as you begin the ascent. It's not just a measly trickle, either – it has stunning miniature waterfalls along its course that make the water foam as it tumbles downwards. Tall pine trees populate this lower landscape too, but not so densely as to obscure all views. In fact, on a clear day you can see the distant peak of the Averau, a huge, pale loaf of rock standing proudly against the blue sky like a lone tooth in a mouth.

The climb's 29 corners are numbered, which is depressing or encouraging depending on your state of mind and the sensations in your legs as you tick them off. What's always motivating, though, is being able to see where you've been. The tightly twisting nature of the Giau means you can look back down on the hairpins you've just ascended, rather than simply worry about what's to come.

If it's hot, there's also some respite in the form of the cool darkness of the avalanche tunnels. These are the best type of tunnels, as they offer a welcome drop in temperature, but still let in natural light thanks to being open on one side, giving you a regular gallery of windows through which to frame mental snapshots of the mountain view as you ride.

Apart from the views, wondering for the umpteenth time if this really is your lowest gear and thinking

about just how good it's going to feel replacing the missing calories, the other common subject to mull over is the history of the climb. You might assume the Giau is a bastion of Giro folklore, a climb that surely Binda, Bartali and Coppi all scaled on their way to a *maglia rosa* or three. But that's not the case.

The Giau wasn't included in the Giro until the race's 56th edition in 1973, when Eddy Merckx won the fourth of his five titles, in so doing completing the first ever Vuelta/Giro double. You can still watch the peloton grinding (the cadences do look remarkably slow by modern standards) up the climb in the wonderful, wistful Jørgen Leth film *Stars and Watercarriers*.

Perhaps even more surprisingly, the Giau wasn't included again for another 16 years, although this might have something to do with the fact that it was only given a layer of tarmac for the first time in 1986. The reason for it being left as gravel for so long is that, despite being a pass, the Giau isn't actually the best way to traverse these mountains: if you want to travel southwest from Cortina d'Ampezzo, the neighbouring and far less steep Passo Falzarego is a more practical option. >>

>> Of course, steep is generally considered good when it comes to bicycle races and so the Giau was back on the Grand Tour menu in 1989, when Laurent Fignon crossed it on his way to his sole Giro win. The Professor would have a rather different experience when the Giau was included for a third time in 1992, the ponytailed Frenchman losing half an hour on the climb as he battled against the weather and hypoglycaemia. It would be another 15 years before the Giau appeared again, in 2007, although it has popped up more regularly since then.

The last couple of kilometres are truly spectacular. A big left-hand hairpin (number 24), about 1,800m (5,905ft) from the top, brings you conclusively into the grassy upland amphitheatre that cradles the summit, and you couldn't wish for a more dramatic climax. As you round the bend and see the full majesty of Mount Nuvolau astride the ridge, it spurs you on to tackle the final few bends that average over 10%. And if the mountain is hidden from view by the weather, there is always the incentive of food from the Berghotel on one side of the road, or the possibility of a divine welcome on the other side in the beautiful little church of Giovanni Gualberto (patron saint of foresters, park rangers and parks).

In Vietnamese, Giàu means rich, and although there's no real translation for the Italian, even without the accent, rich is a fitting description. It might not be the longest or, as it turns out, the most historic climb you ever take on, but it packs so much scenery and altitude into its length that it's well worth the effort it takes to get to the top.

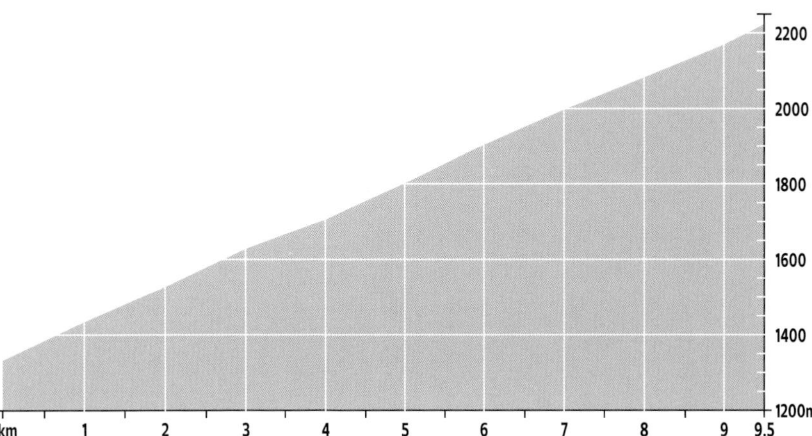

Zoncolan

So steep it reduces pros to a crawl, the Zoncolan in northeast Italy is a true monster of a climb.

It's not often that you associate smells with climbs, but a particular aroma will lodge itself in your memory bank under the letter Z. Alongside all the sights and painful feelings you might reasonably be expected to link inextricably with the Zoncolan is a sweet, slightly sickly, but curiously not unpleasant stink.

The smell is more prevalent towards the bottom of the climb; it comes in waves, lingering for a few laboured pedal strokes at a time as you pass through the miasma. You can tell when it's coming, too, >>

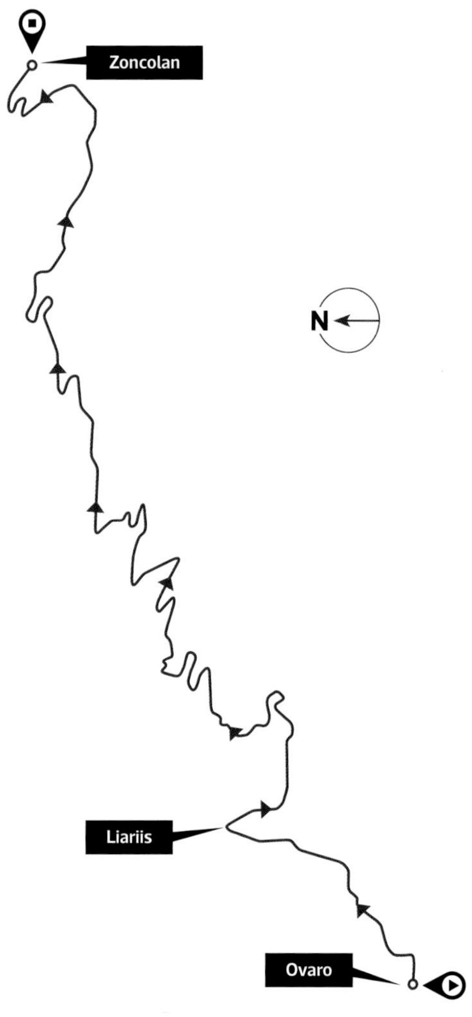

Summit height: 1,730m *(5,676ft)*
Altitude gain: 1,200m *(3,937ft)*
Length: 10.1km *(6¼ miles)*
Average gradient: 11.9%
Maximum gradient: 22%

>> because it is preceded by the sight of a motor vehicle moving very cautiously, creeping around the corners, its driver combatting the severity of the descent by leaning constantly on their brake pedal. And thus the stench of hot pads and discs wafts over you as they drive down the hideously steep incline that you're trying to pedal up.

The Zoncolan was introduced to the wider cycling world as an Italian riposte in the tit-for-tat gradient war between the Giro d'Italia and Vuelta a España, the two Grand Tours battling for the title of most-talked-about race after the one around France. After Italy had struck, perhaps unwittingly, with the Mortirolo in 1990, the Vuelta countered with the Angliru in 2000, before the Giro introduced the Zoncolan in 2003.

Measured from the turning off the SR355 onto the SP123 all the way to the top, the figures for the climb are daunting: 10.1km (6¼ miles) at an average gradient of 11.9%. However, as is so often the case, even these numbers don't tell the full story, because there is a long 6-km (3¾-mile) stretch right in the middle of the climb that averages a horrific 15%, spiking up to 22%.

The Zoncolan is so steep that you feel you're fighting the incline with your whole body

Best not to think too much about what lies ahead as you pedal out of the small town of Ovaro, in the far northeast of Italy. In fact, the start is quite friendly as the first thing that greets you is a big wooden rainbow-shaped arch that declares 'Zoncolan', as if you're entering a theme park. Then, there is a chance to offer up a final prayer for good legs as you pass between the parish church (dedicated to the Holy Trinity) and its *campanile* on the other side of the road.

After that, it's a bit of a leg stretch up to the village of Liariis, where you turn right in the main square. It's a pretty collection of houses, some very Italian and plenty of others more Austrian/Swiss in design, reflecting your proximity to the border. Sitting on benches outside doors will most likely be a few elderly residents who, although giving the appearance of dozing, will no doubt be critiquing your style.

The road flattens briefly as it squeezes between more houses, but then the buildings dwindle and the trees appear. Now you're into those six savage kilometres. There are hairpins, but the type where the gradient seems to kick up viciously rather than flatten out kindly as you switch direction.

The trees were cut back from the immediate sides of the road some years ago, to allow helicopters to film from above during races, but the dense woodland on either side of you still seems oppressive, and the thick air on a hot day can be stultifying. This sense of being hemmed in is also accentuated by the walls that line the hairpins, trapping you on the tarmac.

There is one all-too-short stretch a little before halfway up where the gradient relaxes to just 8%, but it's more of a mental than a physical hiatus, too short to sluice any lactic acid from your muscles. And it won't just be quads and hamstrings crying, 'Enough!' because the Zoncolan is so steep that you feel like you're fighting the incline with your whole body. Triceps soon begin to burn and shoulders start to wilt

as your upper body is called upon to help haul the bike up the strenuous slope. Even your ears are likely to pop as the air thins.

It has sometimes been said that the Zoncolan is actually too steep for real racing – the argument being that there can be no tactics on something this relentlessly steep; no bluffing, nowhere to hide. Chris Froome's victory atop Zoncolan on Stage 14 of the 2018 Giro is often overlooked thanks to his stunning descent on the Colle delle Finestre six days later, but his battle with Simon Yates was a vivid example of just how sheer the climb is. Froome's attack, when it came, had the usual high-cadence hallmarks, but seemed to be taking place in slow motion, and when Yates chased after him they both seemed to be battling through treacle. When a climb makes the pros look slow, you know it's truly tough, and when you pass the turn for the Agriturismo Malga Pozof you will have reached the end of possibly the hardest 6km ($3\frac{3}{4}$ miles) in professional cycling. Thankfully, what follows is well worth the effort.

The final 2km ($1\frac{1}{4}$ miles) begins with a lovely easing of the gradient to something in single figures. Then, the curtain of trees is drawn back and you're presented with a glorious view to your right that reveals just >>

>> how high you've climbed. Next up on the list of rewards is a pair of tunnels that are like a dip in a pool after sunbathing for too long, each providing a few blissfully cooling metres of shade.

After these delights, the final four hairpins, steep though they are, seem much less daunting. The end is in sight and it's a perfect amphitheatre for a finish.

Emerging from the relative silence of the second tunnel into the cauldron of noise created by the expectant *tifosi* waiting on the final switchbacks during an edition of the Giro must be akin to what gladiators felt stepping into the Colosseum.

Finally, it's all over. Once you've caught your breath, you can enjoy one of the best views from any climb anywhere, with a near-360-degree outlook over the peaks of the Carnic Alps. Despite its brutal nature for the bulk of the climb, the Zoncolan is so stunning at the top that it sticks in the memory for more than just the painful pedal strokes needed to conquer it. Sticks in the nostrils,too, of course.

1800
1600
1400
1200
1000
800
600
400m
0km
1
2
3
4
5
6
7
8
9
10.1

Summit height: 2,176m *(7,139ft)*
Altitude gain: 1,695m *(5,561ft)*
Length: 17.8km *(11 miles)*
Average gradient: 9%
Maximum gradient: 14%

Colle delle Finestre

Famed for its 8km (5 miles) of gravel near the summit, the Finestre in northwest Italy provides a memorable challenge for daytrippers and seasoned pros alike.

Theoretically, you get the worst part out of the way first. As you head from the town of Susa to the small neighbouring village of Meana di Susa, the road ramps up to a gradient of 14%, a figure that it will not reach again over the remaining 18km (11 miles) to the summit of the Colle delle Finestre. Practically, however, the need to get out of the saddle in the second kilometre is unlikely to be the effort that you look back on as causing the most discomfort.

For one, it's entirely likely that at this early stage of the climb you're being cajoled by coffee or even powered by pizza, because Susa, approximately 50km (31 miles) west of Turin, is a fine place to grab a bite to eat. Then there is the fact that you may well be slightly distracted from any early discomfort by the challenge of navigating through the narrow streets of Meana di Susa. Signs point the way, but you may feel a little dizzy until you enter the woods. As the houses recede and the trees take over, you can find a gear, get comfortable and, hopefully, settle into a sustainable pace.

Although the gradient is steep, averaging around 10% for this first half, it is at least consistent, because this was built as a military road, albeit at a time when that meant horses and not tanks. That means it's also narrow, and the dense green tunnel created by the leaves can be quite disorientating, particularly when the hairpins begin in earnest.

The Finestre might be best known for its rougher-surfaced second half, but the initial tarmac section is pretty extraordinary, too. About 5km (3 miles) into the climb there's one of the most incredibly intense concentrations of switchbacks you'll ever see. The road accordions up the side of the mountain, packing 29 hairpins into just over 3km (1¾ miles) and 300m (984ft) of altitude gain. There's only about 50m (55yd) of straight road between some of the corners and it was here on Stage 19 that Simon Yates's grip on the 2018 Giro d'Italia began to loosen.

With Team Sky drilling it on the front, it must have been punishing for the British Michelton-Scott rider knowing how much further there was to go on the climb, let alone the stage, when he was dropped. What's more, the continual hairpins combined with >>

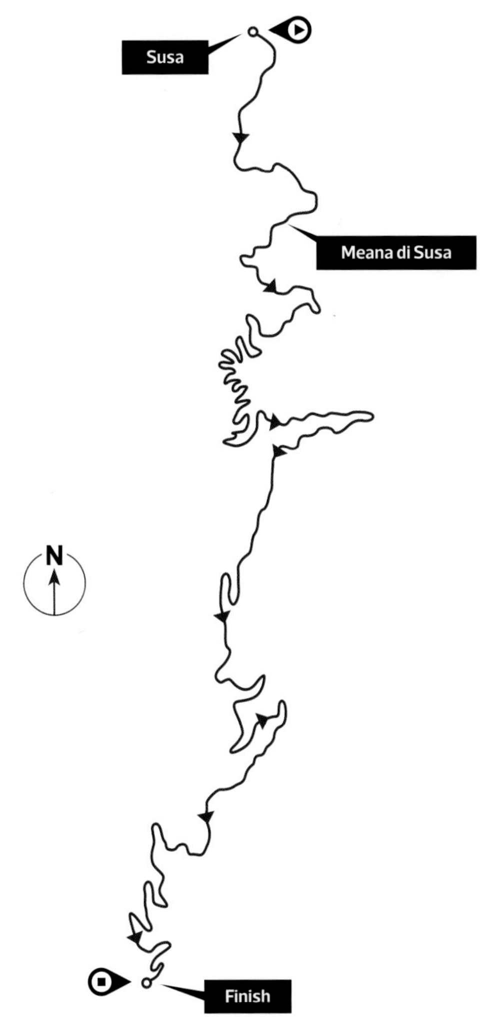

The best time to visit would seem to be a nice dry period in the lead up to the Giro

>> the narrow road exaggerated the natural concertina effect on the peloton, with those swinging at the back (like Yates in the leader's pink jersey) worst off.

There are three relatively straight kilometres (1¾ miles) between the top of this dizzying section and the end of the tarmac. As you emerge from the hairpins, you get the first real idea of altitude gained, as there are gaps between the trees to your left, like windows (or *finestre* in Italian) allowing you to look out onto the Susa valley.

Just before you hit the gravel, you'll see a white building on the right and a wooden sign on the left. Then, in an instant, the sound from your tyres will change and the chain will begin to rattle. There is no gradual increase in hostilities – it's just a clear-cut line. One minute you're on tarmac, the next you're not.

The actual severity of the surface will depend on conditions on the day. The best time to visit would seem to be during a nice dry period in the lead-up to the Giro passing through. Looking back at the footage from that astounding day in 2018, you can see that by the time Team Sky's last pacemaker teammate peeled off the front, Chris Froome was already more than two and a half minutes ahead of Yates, who was only just transitioning from sealed to unsealed surface. However, the footage also shows that the ground that both riders experienced that day was relatively smooth, compacted, almost polished and swept clear of loose stones.

Depending on the number of vehicles that have been using it, the road can get quite chopped up. Throw in some rain and things get even worse. A liberal scattering of stones across the road, sandy ruts on the hairpins and the washboard-like surface on the entry and exit of corners, caused by cars and trucks braking heavily and repeatedly, will take their toll. >>

>> Although the gradient on this second half averages a slightly milder 9%, the energy-sapping surface, the extra balance required to constantly adjust your line to avoid rocks and the accumulated fatigue can certainly make it feel steeper than advertised. It's also mentally demanding having to constantly focus on picking the right line, although at times this is like queuing in traffic on a motorway or freeway. You always think the other lane is the faster one.

Initially, the trees – mostly pines here – persist on either side, but gradually they diminish in number and the views on a sunny day are glorious. The weather can, of course, set a different, more misty, muted and monochromatic sort of mood. Yet this can feel appropriate, because when the Giro first came here in 2005 the Italian television directors got so excited by the dramatic, 'timeless' scenes on the climb that they turned the pictures black and white.

Whether the hardest part is at the start is debatable, but with its final flurry of gravelly hairpins there's no question that the climb saves the best part until last. Danilo Di Luca was first over the summit that day in 2005 and at the top there is a slightly odd stone relief of the man to commemorate his achievement.

Although relatively high at 2,176m (7,139ft), according to the signs, it's a small summit, certainly not big enough to host a stage finish. Yet the Finestre has produced some memorable moments in the few races it has hosted, and while it doesn't lie that far from major French climbs, such as the Izoard, Iseran and Galibier, it is nonetheless very Italian in nature and there's a quiet remoteness to it that's exacerbated by the gravel section. Even on a grim day, this ascent is a magical experience that will make you vow to return.

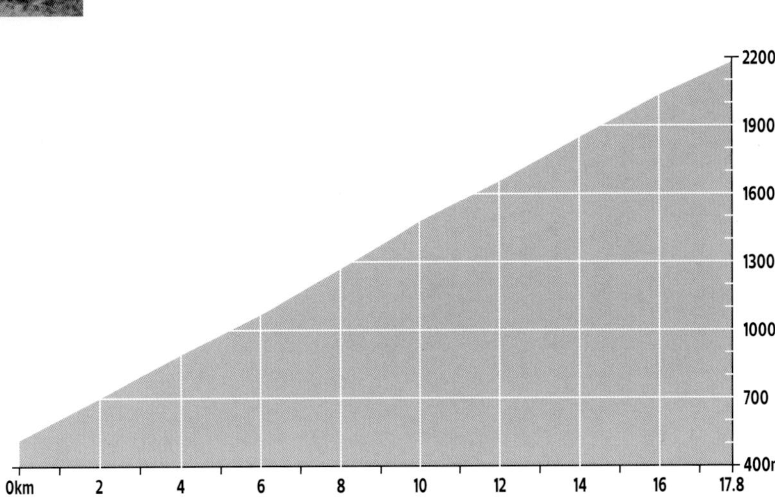

Summit height: 2,757m *(9,045ft)*
Altitude gain: 1,841m *(6,040ft)*
Length: 24.1km *(15 miles)*
Average gradient: 8%
Maximum gradient: 11%

Passo dello Stelvio

It has the beauty, the heritage and the hairpins...lots and lots of hairpins. This makes the Stelvio – in our opinion – the greatest climb of them all.

More than 200 years ago – and around 60 years before the bicycle as we know it was invented – work began on possibly the most famous mountain pass on Earth. Holy Roman Emperor Francis II wanted to connect the Austrian crown land of Tyrol with its new territory in Lombardy, which it had acquired in the Congress of Vienna. He commissioned Italian engineer Carlo Donegani to build the Stilfser Joch, which is what we now know in Italian as the Passo dello Stelvio.

The name is taken from the town at the start of the northeastern side of the pass, Prad am Stilfserjoch or Prato allo Stelvio (and they are in that order on the bilingual signs, as most of the population speaks German). Setting out from here, the 24.1-km (15-mile) climb begins relatively gently. In fact, given that pretty much every photo ever published of the Stelvio shows a plethora of hairpins, you might begin to wonder after a while if you're on the right road.

Up the valley you have the waters of the Trafoier Bach babbling away next to you. So closely do road and river mirror each other that it's like the watery other half of a dual carriageway, first on your right and then, after about 3km (1¾ miles), on your left. It peels away briefly as you reach Gomagoi, then rejoins. But still no switchbacks.

It's only as you emerge from an avalanche tunnel around 7km (4⅓ miles) into the ride that the SS38 first doubles back on itself. It's an impressive first effort too, with the road sitting proud of a big stone wall, creating a balcony effect. It then zags to counter the first zig and it's another 2km (1¼ miles) before the next pair of hairpins arrives, in Trafoi. It's a curious start, then. After 10km (6¼ miles) of the total climb, just four of the 48 hairpins have been tackled and the gradient has averaged around 6%.

Next come the trees. For about 6km (3¾ miles) you ride up between dark green needles, and while the hairpins now arrive in earnest, the views are fairly fleeting. The gradient is now closer to 9%, which >>

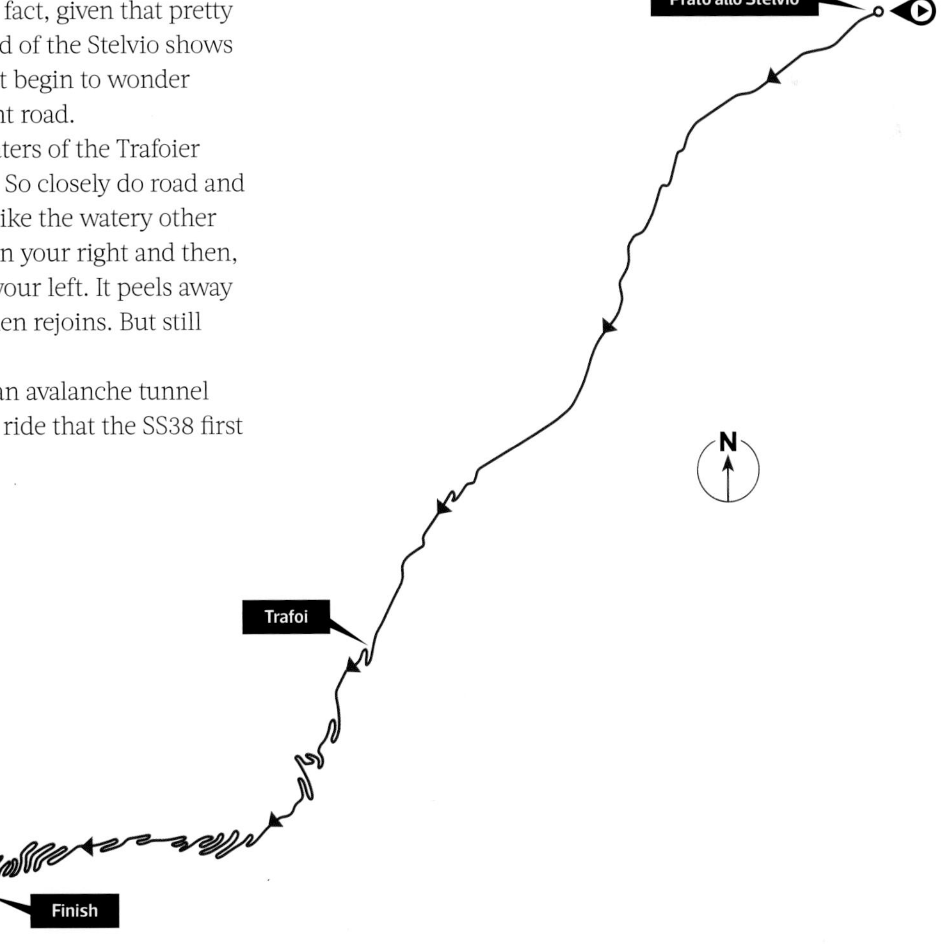

>> will start you thinking about the times that a professional peloton has passed this way.

The top of the road stands at a breezy 2,757m (9,045ft) in altitude, meaning it was the highest pass in the Alps for well over a century until the Col de l'Iseran opened and pipped it by just 7m (23ft). The Iseran made its debut in a Grand Tour just a year after it was opened, in the Tour de France of 1938, yet curiously the Stelvio didn't appear in the Giro d'Italia until 1953.

The Italian climb's Grand Tour premiere was the scene of a drama befitting the scale of its slopes, however. Swiss rider Hugo Koblet was leading overall on Stage 20 and, having kept four-time Giro winner Fausto Coppi at bay on the previous day's mountain stage, looked as though he would emerge victorious in Milan. In fact, it was claimed by some that a truce had been agreed between the two protagonists before the penultimate stage.

Koblet, however, was showing signs of weakness as they reached the Stelvio, so one of Coppi's domestiques, Andrea Carrea, began to set a furious pace. Yet it was Koblet who arguably broke any truce first. Just after Carrea had swung off the front, job done, an attack was put in (at Coppi's behest) by a young rider named Nino Defilippis, whom Koblet chased down and went past. Coppi counterattacked, however, and proceeded to pass both of them 'like a motorbike', according to Defilippis. The Italian great took victory not only on the stage but in the race as Koblet crashed twice on the descent and lost three and a half minutes. Their friendship was over.

It's fitting that when the Cima Coppi prize (awarded to the first rider to the highest point of the Giro) was introduced in 1965, the Stelvio was that race's zenith. Less fittingly, it was one of the occasions when snow was still lying thickly on the slopes of the climb, so although the riders didn't have to give it a miss as they did in 1988 and 2013, the finish line was nonetheless brought down to just under 2,000m (6,562ft).

With 17.5km (11 miles) and 28 about-turns behind you, the daunting denouement of the climb comes into view. A stack of switchbacks scales the wall at the end of the valley, a helter-skelter of hairpins that looks all at once horrendous and heavenly.

It might not register as you contemplate the 500m (1,640ft) of vertical ascent to come, but there is an aspect of the Stelvio that really deserves praise from an aesthetic perspective. The drops at the side of the >>

At a breezy 2,757m (9,045ft), the pass was the highest in the Alps for over a century

>> road mean that a barrier of some sort is necessary to mitigate against fatigued cyclists and absent-minded motorists simply wobbling off the edge. But instead of some ugly metal Armco, there are low stone walls that look like castellations hewn sympathetically from the landscape. It bolsters the impression that you are entering some sort of mountain fortress.

The steepness of the climb and the lack of trees up high mean it's easy to look over the ramparts to the road unfurling beneath you. It's not quite as encouraging looking down as it is intimidating looking up, but it's still a fillip as you tick off the kilometres. Depending on whether your bidon is half empty or half full, the *tornati* are either irritating as they upset your rhythm or a nice way of breaking up the climb by giving you small targets to aim for. If you weren't born in Colombia, you'll notice the thinner air as you climb this final stretch, too.

You reach the summit of this wild and inspiring road only to discover that in the last 200 years a large number of buildings have been built. Some are hotels but most are shops trying to take advantage of oxygen-starved minds by selling commemorative tat. Better to turn your back on it all and look down upon the beauty of the road you've just climbed.

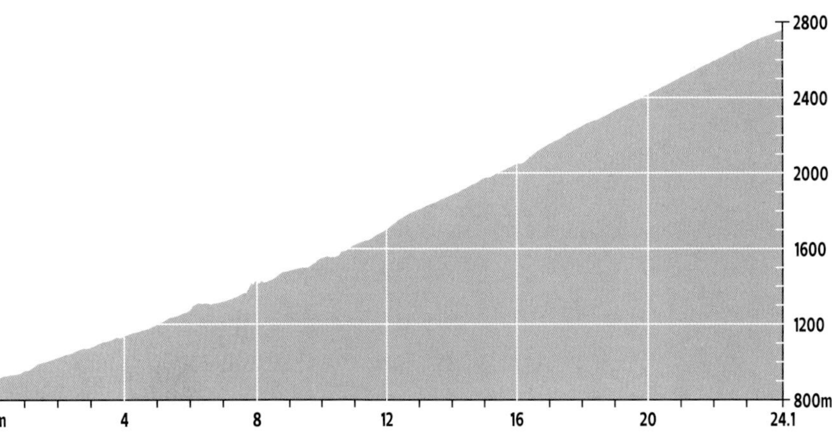

Passo Gavia

Beautiful yet daunting, the Gavia secured its notoriety on one brutal day at the Giro d'Italia in 1988.

Wild. That's the best word to sum up the Passo Gavia in northern Italy. Wild because of the sense that nature doesn't really want a road up there, and wild because of that famous photo of Andy Hampsten in the snow. And yet, if you set out from Ponte di Legno expecting that word to define the whole climb, you'd be rather perplexed after the first kilometre. In fact, after 6km (3¾ miles) of wide, smooth road that has only risen at an average of 6% you might be thinking of another word. Tame.

Then, like Clark Kent removing his specs, the whole character of the road changes. One moment you're on a hairpin with airy views of mountains and a white line down the middle of the tarmac, the next you're on a single-track road with trees shutting out the light as though you've entered a narrow tunnel. From this point onwards, you are forced to concentrate harder, initially because the road is so slender that it feels like even the briefest moment's inattention could see you teeter over the edge. If you encounter a car, it can be a squeeze to fit both vehicles side by side.

After 2km (1¼ miles) and four hairpins on this confined corridor, the trees recede and although the road doesn't gain any more breadth, there's a sense of relief as the views open out around you and the light returns. It's like curtains being drawn back on the ultimate picture window at the end of a hallway. Unless it's snowing.

In 1988, Stage 14 of the Giro d'Italia was 120km (74½ miles) long, which in those days seemed remarkably short for a mountain stage. But there was nothing meagre about it. The Gavia had first been a part of the Giro in 1960, but stages that included this climatically capricious pass had been cancelled in 1961 and 1984. Many argued it should be struck from the route in 1988 too, but race director Vincenzo Torriani insisted the show must go on. As a result, the most famous photo from the day shows US rider Hampsten with snow covering his hair and shoulders, big Oakley sunglasses looking more like ski goggles than ever as he battles up the freezing climb.

Look more closely and you'll see that he was actually quite well prepared, with thick gloves and yellow lenses in the glasses. In other photos, he has a woolly hat on (likely bought along with the gloves that morning by his 7-Eleven team, who made a dash >>

Summit height: 2,621m *(8,599ft)*
Altitude gain: 1,363m *(4,472ft)*
Length: 17.3km *(10¾ miles)*
Average gradient: 7.9%
Maximum gradient: 16%

>> for a ski shop when warned of the weather) and long sleeves under the thick wool Castelli blue jersey that he was wearing as leader of the combined classification.By comparison, photos of the rider first to the top, Johan van der Velde, show the Dutchman with no gloves and bare arms. He could only look more inappropriately attired if he was pushing the pedals in flip-flops. It's perhaps no wonder that on the descent to Bormio, Hampsten and many others would pass van der Velde, who actually walked back up the mountain at one point in search of anything warming. He eventually finished 47 minutes down.

Hampsten gained enough time on his rivals to take the leader's pink jersey, which he would wear all the way to Milan. But although he won the race overall, he is remembered more for his ride on Stage 14 – 'The Day the Big Men Cried', as *La Gazzetta dello Sport* christened it.

Thankfully, most of us have more choice when it comes to picking a day to ride the Gavia, and if you choose well you'll enjoy some wonderful vistas. Most of the time you'll be looking ahead, of course, but there are opportunities to look over the vertiginous verges back down onto the road below.

After a flurry of hairpins the road runs relatively straight for about 3.5km (2¼ miles), but it still seems tiny, teetering like a little ledge high up on the right-hand side of the huge valley. Even if you don't have a fear of heights, the fact that you are over 2,100m (6,890ft) high may well start to take its toll on your cardiovascular system.

And then there's the tunnel with just over 3km (1¾ miles) to go. Although there are lights inside, it still feels oppressively dark, and a rear light is a good >>

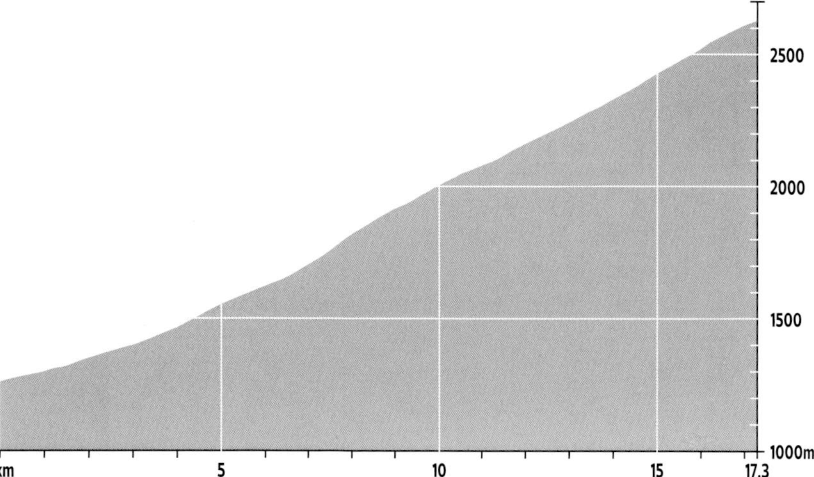

A trio of hairpins makes for a steep and spectacular final flourish with precarious views

>> idea for peace of mind. And while it's only 500m (1/3 mile) in length, it seems to last an eternity thanks to a gradient of over 9%. It's worth persevering through the darkness though, because the final few kilometres to the summit are some of the most beautiful of the climb. The road is rough (although it was just dirt in 1988) and the landscape raw, but there's an untamed ruggedness that makes it feel timeless. The Lago Nero appears off to the side of the road. It's one half of a pair, the other being the Lago Bianco just beyond the summit. Legends vary, but essentially they are said to represent two young lovers separated by evil.

A trio of hairpins hacked into the rock makes for a steep and spectacular final flourish with precarious views back down the road you've just climbed. Then, you turn your back on the Valle delle Messi and enter a more mellow bowl. Over the last 600m (656yd), a long right-hand curve delivers you relatively gently to the liberally stickered sign at the summit, from where you can trot up onto a ridge nearby to see the statue of the Madonna delle Vette, the cyclists' protector and patron saint.

Two other frozen faces stare out over the climb. One is a slightly cartoonish visage of Fausto Coppi, which might seem slightly odd as the Italian great died before the climb was included in the Giro. However, the climb has been the site of the Cima Coppi, or highest point of the Giro, several times. The other bust is of Torriani, the suave, chain-smoking Giro race director who first brought the Gavia into the race in 1960 and then sealed the climb's place in history with his decision to run that famous stage over it on 5th June 1988.

It would be his last Giro in charge. A wild decision. A wild climb.

Colle del Nivolet

Hidden away in the northwest corner of Italy is a climb of such grand scale and rare beauty it's a wonder that more people don't know about it.

As the bus swerves down the hillside, the occupants are flung from side to side at each hairpin bend. The large stack of stolen gold slides across the floor until eventually the rear end of the bus skids off the road and is left hanging precariously over the void below. With the heavy stash of gold threatening to tip the bus and its passengers into the abyss, Michael Caine delivers one of the most famous final lines in movie history: 'Hang on a minute, lads, I've got a great idea.'

That scene in Peter Collinson's *The Italian Job* was shot on the slopes of the Colle del Nivolet. Michael Caine and his gang were supposed to be escaping over the Alps after pulling off a heist in Turin, except that if they were actually on the Nivolet then they were most certainly going the wrong way.

The Colle del Nivolet is a road to nowhere, only built to service the dam at Lago Serrù and provide tourist access to the Gran Paradiso National Park. The road peters out a short distance beyond the summit and from there you'll need to don walking boots and crampons if you want to escape over the border into France. (As an aside, if you did trek across those border peaks, you'd find yourself at the top of another classic climb, the Col de l'Iseran, but you definitely wouldn't be reaching it by bicycle.)

The Nivolet's narrow, winding road is no place for buses, and its summit barely has space for cars to do a U-turn, which goes some way to explaining why it has been largely ignored by the Giro d'Italia – there just isn't room to set up a summit finish. But that's all for the best, because its lack of notoriety means you won't have to share your space with hordes of other cyclists chasing the best time, and you can enjoy the beauty of the climb in splendid isolation.

Mind you, it's hard to say where the Colle del Nivolet actually starts. If you wanted, you could start in Turin and be climbing on a single road for the best part of 100km (62 miles) – however, most people set off from the small town of Locana, which is the last settlement of any size before the road heads into the wilds of the Graian Alps. >>

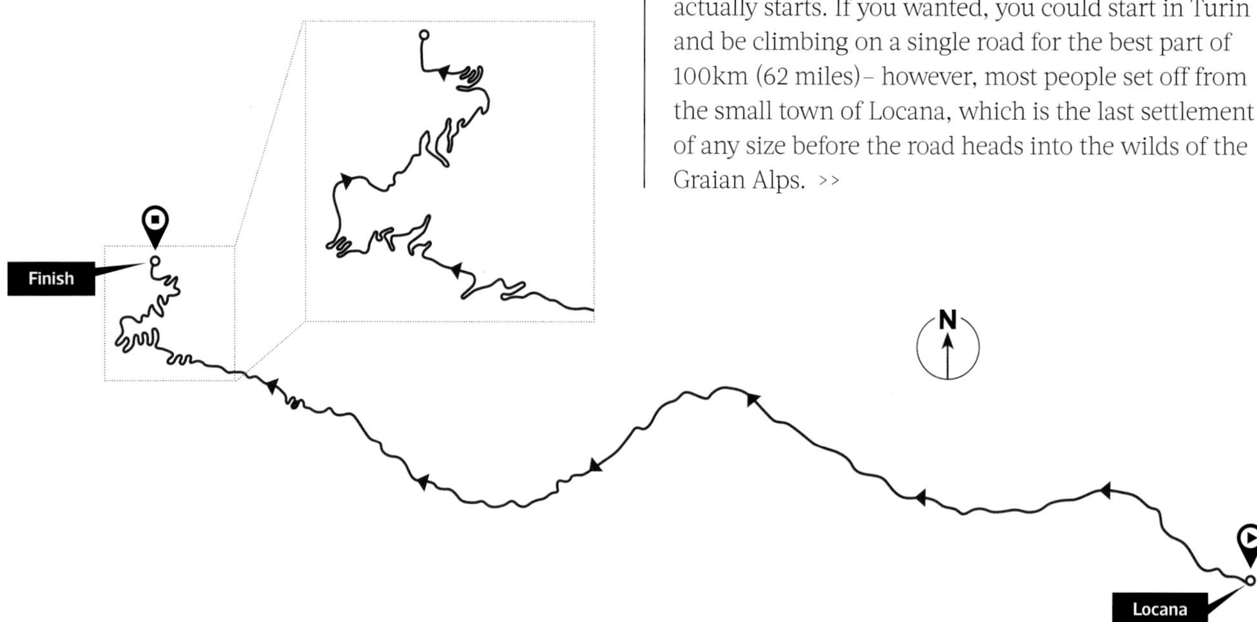

Summit height: 2,612m *(8,570ft)*
Altitude gain: 1,999m *(6,558ft)*
Length: 40km *(25 miles)*
Average gradient: 4.9%
Maximum gradient: 15%

>> From Locana, it's 40km (25 miles) to the top, nearly all of it uphill. You simply point yourself in a westerly direction and keep going. The first 14km ($8\frac{3}{4}$ miles) meander upwards at a gentle gradient; so gentle, in fact, you could be forgiven for thinking you were on the flat. It's only the heavy feeling in your legs that gives away the fact that you're gaining height. It's also during this phase that you come to a worrying realization: the 4.9% average gradient is not spread evenly throughout the climb. These early slopes of 1–2% are an indicator that things will get steep later on.

Actually, things get steep very quickly. Just as you're enjoying ambling through a lush valley next to a

Just before the summit, you'll be rewarded with one of the finest views in cycling

lazy river, passing occasional farmsteads and holiday homes, the road suddenly lurches to the right and you're faced with a flurry of hairpins at 15%. Once you struggle past them, you immediately arrive at a fresh obstacle: a 3.5-km ($2^1/_4$-mile) tunnel, which itself includes some pretty severe gradients, only this time they need to be tackled in the dark.

Fortunately, there's an escape road to the side of the tunnel, which is a bit gravelly and potholed in places, but is much more pleasant than grinding uphill in a tunnel as fast as you can while praying that a coachload of Michael Caine fans doesn't come barrelling through at the same time.

Beyond the tunnel, the route returns to more bucolic meandering beside rivers and lakes, with families enjoying picnics in the sunshine, until you arrive at kilometre 27 (mile 17). That's where the road swings abruptly away from the valley and you find yourself venturing upwards into a different world.

From here, the gradients get steeper and the landscape more dramatic. The gentle fields are replaced by rock-strewn hillsides and the trees give way to hardier grasses and ferns. Dark mountains loom ahead, their flanks covered with snow even at the height of summer.

After 7km ($4^1/_3$ miles), the road arrives at the imposing stone wall of the Serrù Dam, which holds back the water that supplies Turin and the surrounding Piedmont region. When the Giro finally visited these slopes, a full 110 years after the first edition of Italy's Grand Tour, this is as far as the race got. On Stage 13 of the 2019 edition, Russia's Ilnur Zakarin won solo at the foot of the great dam. While it's certain that the riders were happy that the finish line wasn't any higher up, it was also a shame for anyone watching the race, because the next bit only gets more beautiful. >>

>> **By now, you're in among mountains that dwarf** everything in their shadow. The road flattens briefly as it passes the icy, turquoise waters of Lago Agnel, before pitching up more steeply again through a series of hairpins that snake between great cliffs of grey rock. Just before the summit, take a peek back over your left shoulder and you'll be rewarded with one of the finest views available to a cyclist: a monumental bowl of rock and ice, peppered with lakes and bisected by a narrow scrawl of tarmac that disappears off into the far distance.

At the top, there is no cafe or gift shop, no monument to Fausto Coppi or car park full of tourist buses, just a sign informing you that you are at 2,612m (8,570ft), almost as high as the Col du Galibier and significantly higher than the likes of the Tourmalet and Mont Ventoux. Then, once you've gorged on the views and given your legs a chance to recover, there's nothing else to do but turn around and let gravity carry you back down for 40 wonderful kilometres (20 miles) and over 2,000 vertical metres (6,562 vertical feet) to Locana. Now that really *is* a great idea.

2500
2000
1500
1000
500m
0km 5 10 15 20 25 30 35 40

Spain

Summit height: 1,570m *(5,151ft)*
Altitude gain: 1,250m *(4,101ft)*
Length: 13.19km *(8¼ miles)*
Average gradient: 9%
Maximum gradient: 29%

Alto de l'Angliru

In northern Spain is a climb of such savagery it has reduced pros to walking up its 20% slopes.

Admittedly, it's akin to the joy of poking yourself in the eye with a spoon rather than a fork, but nonetheless there is a 16% pitch near the top of the Angliru that feels blissful. Despite the fact that the tarmac is rearing towards the heavens at a gradient more severe than anything you will find on the Galibier, Stelvio, Ventoux or Alpe d'Huez, this portion of Spain's toughest climb actually serves as respite after the hellish section preceding it.

That is exactly the sort of diabolical theatre that Unipublic – organizer of the Vuelta a España before ASO took over in 2014 – was looking for in the late 1990s. The man who found the climb was Miguel Prieto, who not only worked for the blind charity Once (sponsors of the hugely successful cycling team) but was partially sighted himself. The 'blind visionary', as he became known, found the recently surfaced cattle track when he was on holiday in the Asturias, and wrote to the men in charge of the Vuelta. >>

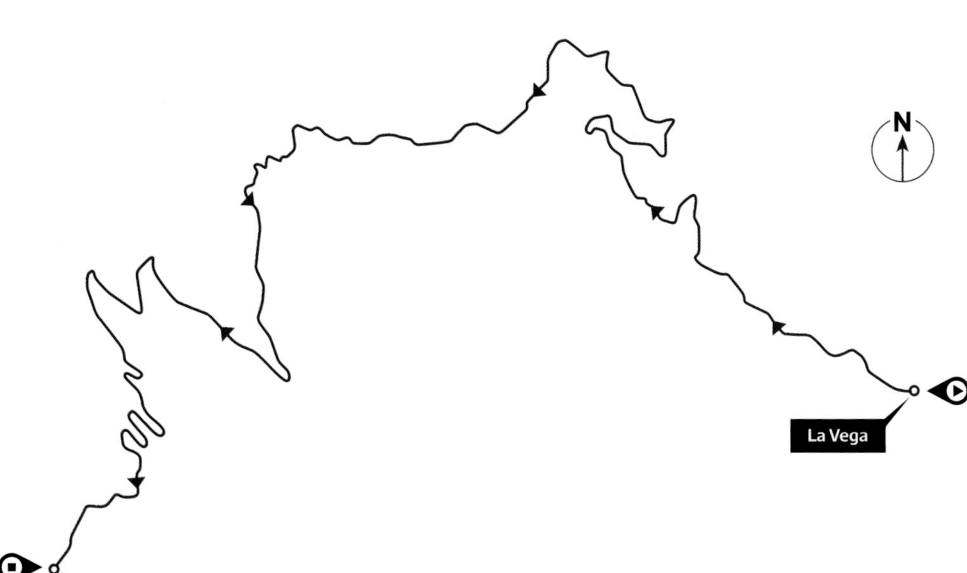

>> At the time, the race was seen as the poor relation to the Tour and Giro, and the Spaniards wanted a climb to rival the reputations of Mont Ventoux and the Mortirolo. The Angliru was just the ticket, and in 1999 it made its debut in Spain's Grand Tour.

Prieto billed it as a climb of 12km ($7^1/_2$ miles), but the modern Strava segment extends to include the final downhill rush to the finish line used in the race, making it 13.19km ($8^1/_4$ miles) at an average of 9%. The first 5km (3 miles) of climbing is a mere softener for the main event – light sparring at single-figure gradients. It still has sustained stretches of 9%, so it's hard to take it easy, yet save as much energy as you can.

The first few kilometres feel rather Italian in nature as they wind through a landscape of rolling, tree-covered hills with terracotta-topped houses dotted across the slopes. Then, at 6km ($3^3/_4$ miles), you reach the interval between the first and second acts. It's a rather lovely linking section that transfers you through some open, bracken-covered heathland with views out across the early slopes you've just scaled. It's also flat. Don't be tempted to rush it, though, because the next 6km ($3^3/_4$ miles) average an intimidating 13% and will hit well over 20% for several sustained stretches.

David Millar famously stopped 1m (3ft) before the finish line and removed his number

It was this next section that caused the controversy in the early years of the Angliru's inclusion in the Vuelta, with some calling it impossible and others saying it was effectively pushing the riders to dope. David Millar famously stopped a metre (3ft) before the finish line and removed his number, disqualifying himself from the 2002 race despite being in the top ten at the time. He was actually protesting at the dangerous descent preceding the Angliru, but one wonders whether he would have been quite so rash if the climb to the line had been a little less punishing.

It probably didn't help that it was wet on the climb that year, and when you're here the idea of your rear wheel slipping will send shivers down your spine. Even in the dry, you will have to avoid slippery sections, because the quiet nature of the climb means that cattle wander up it and occasionally use it as something of a livestock latrine.

The first beastly stretch of over 20% extends through a handful of hairpins and, because you've just had a rest on the flat section, it seems horrible but not horrific. What it does do is wake up your arms, core and back muscles. Climbing these sorts of gradients feels like a whole-body workout as sinews strain in everything from forehead to fingertip.

The hardest section by far is La Cueña les Cabres, which extends between two hairpins about 10km ($6^1/_4$ miles) into the climb and has spikes of nearly 30%. As you round the hairpin at its start, the road stretches out in front of you like a staircase with no steps.

If you're struggling to raise your gaze from your stem, the start is signposted by a sculpture that looks as though the Tin Man from *The Wizard of Oz* has died while attempting to cycle up it, possibly going so slowly that he simply rusted to a halt. The transition >>

1600
1400
1200
1000
800
600
400
200m
0km
2
4
6
8
10
12
13.19

>> from sitting in the saddle to standing on the pedals is so tricky on this sort of gradient that you risk stalling and having to put a foot down. Equally, the road feels too narrow and cambered to make weaving a viable option. There is nowhere to hide.

It's no consolation while embroiled in your own fight against gravity, but even the pros look like they're going in slow motion up this stretch. Juan José Cobo (in 2011, when he emerged from obscurity to beat Chris Froome and Bradley Wiggins into second and third place respectively) is perhaps the only one who has ever made this pitch look manageable.

Then you reach that blissful 16%. The pain isn't over because the road ramps up again a few more times, but somehow the summit feels reachable now. If you can beat La Cueña les Cabres, you can beat anything.

The downhill denouement that comes a little while later feels odd. As you flash across the finish line, you realize it's a rather pointless climb, because there's nothing at the top – no hotel, no cafe, not even really any view, just a car park that is presumably only as large as it is to service the Vuelta circus. There's a couple of monuments and a peaceful landscape of green and grey over which you can stare and contemplate the climb you've just completed.

As the sound of raging blood dissipates, you realize what a quiet place it is. And as you descend a few minutes later you notice, possibly for the first time, that there's more to the Angliru than the gradient. Released by gravity from the painful climbing hunch that restricts your vision to a narrow tunnel, you look out over the most wonderfully expansive view, with Oviedo below and the Bay of Biscay beyond. The climb might be cruel, but the Angliru is a beast that is also rather beautiful.

Descending, there is a wonderfully expansive view to Oviedo and to the Bay of Biscay beyond

Alto de Velefique

It has the length, the height and the hairpins, yet this climb in southern Spain is wonderfully off the beaten track.

Unless you have a horse with no name, you'll be driving through the Tabernas Desert to reach the start of this climb. This arid southeastern knuckle of Spain is so quintessential in its desertedness it became the home of cowboy movies in the 1960s. It would take many hours to cycle here from anywhere you would wish to base yourself in the vicinity. But there are roads, and what roads they are.

The sun beats all year round. The nights are cold whatever the season – candy-striped snow poles line the highest roads – but even in late October the temperature is still in the low 30s C (high 80s F) during the day. This consistent dry warmth coupled with the near-total lack of motor traffic means the tarmac tends to stay in fine fettle, unfurling like black linoleum across the desert sand. And of those roads there is none so beautiful to a cyclist as Alto de Velefique.

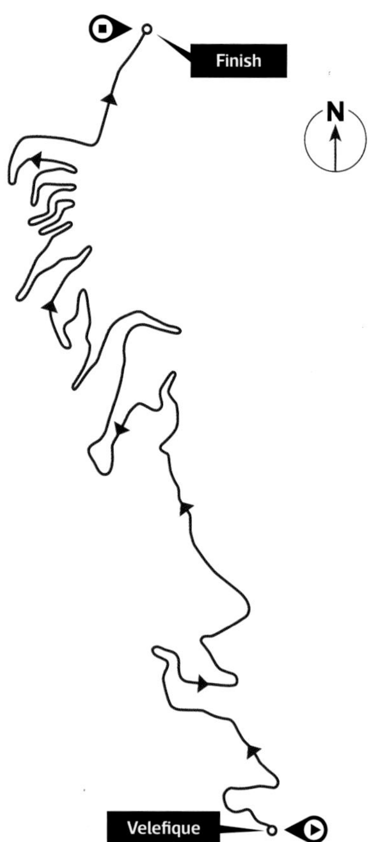

Ask any local rider and the word 'Velefique' is met with the reverential pronouncement, 'Ah, the Alpe d'Huez of the desert,' and they're not wrong. Both climbs top out at a similar height, reached over a similar distance, and Velefique has 20 perfect hairpins, just one shy of the infamous Alpe (see page 120). The two climbs even look similar on a map, running south to north like film spooling off a reel. But in terms of feel the two couldn't be more different, not least because riders on Alpe d'Huez probably outnumber those on the Velefique by a thousand to one.

The technical term here is 'semi-arid', which means there's slightly more precipitation than a full-blown 'arid' desert, but not much. It's more pleasant to stay on the east coast, where bustling towns abound an hour's drive away. Then, as you might have guessed, the climb proper gets underway on the outskirts of Velefique, a tiny old mining town.

The road is the AL-3102 but you needn't worry, it's basically the only road running north and there are plenty of signs. First up is one for cyclists, a full course profile plus stats. It declares numbers you will disagree with by the top. According to the sign's writers, the Velefique crests at 1,860m (6,102ft), with an average gradient of 7.95% and a maximum of 11%. But by the third hairpin you'll have seen your bike computer whizz past 11%, and by the summit you'll be sitting on your top tube at a shade under 1,800m (5,900ft). It's the same phenomenon that led France's Cime de la Bonette to declare itself '2,802m (9,193ft) above >>

Summit height: 1,789m *(5,869½ft)*
Altitude gain: 894m *(2,933ft)*
Length: 12.42km *(7¾ miles)*
Average gradient: 7.2%
Maximum gradient: 13%

DECCA

>> sea level, the highest road in Europe', when in fact that award belongs to another Spanish queen, the 3,398m (11,148ft) Pico de Veleta.

Past the sign, a cluster of whitewashed houses springs into view and with it the first hairpin, which whisks you out of the prickly pears that flank the roadside and into a spray of colour. Velefique's inhabitants are clearly into their ornamental flowers. It's an enormously steep sweep, then another, and by the fourth the village exists only over your right shoulder.

Rhythm is easy to find, so too evidence that you are not the first rider to have realized that this is a magnificent climb. Faded Albertos, Valverdes and Javis crisscross the road, graffitied relics of Vueltas past – although in Grand Tour terms Alto de Velefique is a long way short of being 'the Alpe d'Huez of the Vuelta a España'.

The caravan first came to town in 2009 for Stage 12, a gruelling 191km (119 miles) from Almería in the south and packing 3,550m (11,647ft) of climbing. Ryder Hesjedal took the first Vuelta stage win for a Canadian and climbed mid-stage, then again last thing as the route looped around for a summit finish. Along with Hesjedal, Velefique was heralded a breakthrough star, yet the race didn't return until 2017.

On a clear day, the view over the desert is far-reaching but by its very nature rather featureless. The middle-distance is yellow and grey, sandy earth and sunburned scrub intertwined with rock, while the horizon has the quality of reddish, wrinkled cloth. It's all very desolate and is the reason the Tabernas Desert became such a favourite for cinema. More recently, leviathans such as *Game of Thrones* have been shot in these parts, but back in the 1960s and 1970s European >>

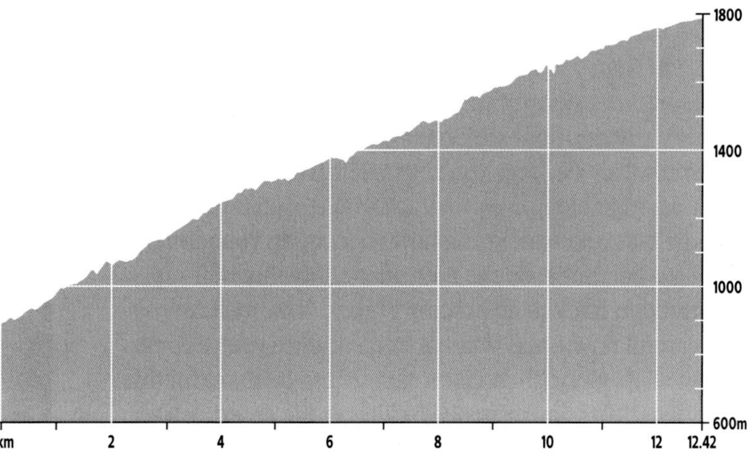

On a clear day, the view over the desert is far reaching but by its very nature rather featureless

>> production companies built vast sets – whole towns complete with courts, bars and cathouses – in which to film Spaghetti Westerns, so-called because they were typically directed by Italians, the most famous being Sergio Leone. At least three of the more major movie sets survive and have been made into tourist attractions, so it's still possible to tread where Clint Eastwood toted his guns in Leone's *Dollars Trilogy*. However, when the landscape takes a marked turn as the hairpins tick by, you will discover a twist in the plot up here, too.

From the beginning of the climb you'd have never known it, but in the coils of hairpins that finally elevate you to the summit there are suddenly huge swathes of conifers, and with them huge blasts of chill air. Rolling through in just a lightweight jersey, you would shiver on some of these upper slopes were it not for the steepened pitches between the hairpins' straighter sections, which are enough to have you adding to the sweat patches. These sections are plentifully long, and between the copses provide the perfect galleries from which to take in the road below. It is a truly magnificent sight, yet one totally eclipsed by that which greets you at the top.

At first, you'll wonder where the grandeur has gone – the summit sees the road appear to dilute flatly into the sky – but seek out another brown sign, which spuriously declares you're at 1,860m (6,102ft), then turn right along a gravel track. You'll soon be ditching the bike and wondering how good a grip your cleats have got, but keep the faith and follow this well-trodden track to an outcrop of rock. Now look over – careful now – and witness from whence you've come in all its glory. Then take a moment to be thankful this incredible climb remains hidden in the desert.

Summit height: 682m *(2,237½ft)*
Altitude gain: 647m *(2,123ft)*
Length: 9.5km *(6 miles) (ascent only)*
Average gradient: 7%
Maximum gradient: 11%

Sa Calobra

Smooth, sinuous and sun-drenched – no road is as tailor-made for cyclists as the legendary Sa Calobra on the island of Mallorca.

There are climbs that are famous for their place in Tour history; climbs that are famous for their extreme height and savagery; climbs that are famous for the splendour of their surroundings. This climb, however, is famous for its road. No other road on the planet can match its joyous swoops and swirls, or the playful way it loops around and under itself like a tie knot.

It's hard to believe that the enigmatic pattern it carves is determined purely by the contours of the hillside and the practical necessities of constructing the most efficient route from bottom to top. It seems certain that when Italian-Spanish engineer Antonio >>

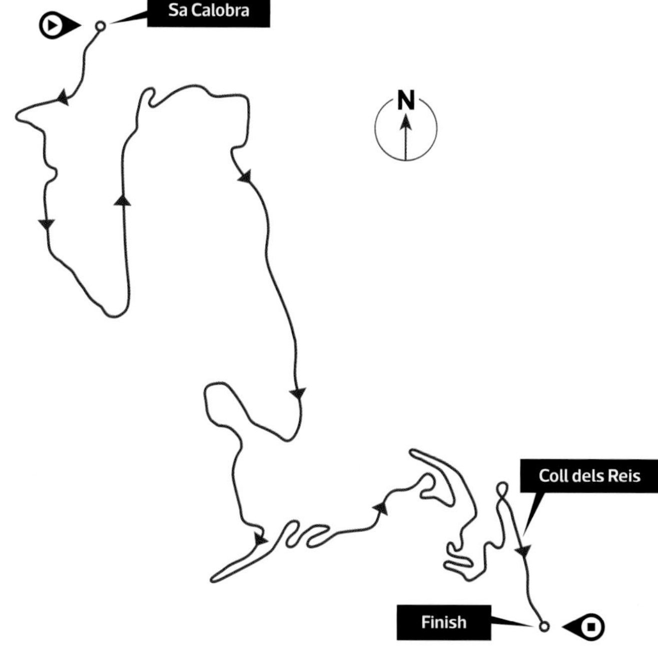

>> Parietti was building the Sa Calobra access road in the early 1930s he saw an opportunity to create something magnificent as well as functional: a road that people would want to visit purely for its own sake rather than for where it might take them.

Parietti may not have had bicycles in mind when he designed his road, but he couldn't have made it more perfect had it magically appeared from the collective dreams of the world's cyclists.

Most climbs are named after whatever lies at their summit, meaning this climb should really be called the Coll dels Reis. It's a fairly insignificant lump on the northern edge of Mallorca, at around only 700m (2,297ft) above sea level, which could explain why the climb is more commonly named after the pretty harbour that sits at its foot, Port de Sa Calobra.

As if to mirror this back-to-front way of doing things, the climb also starts at the top. The only way to ascend Sa Calobra is to descend it first. After leaving the Ma-10 main road and stopping for coffee at the Cafe Escorca, you make your way up to Coll dels Reis from the southern side. At the top a short alleyway carved through a rocky outcrop merely serves to add to the drama. It's like coming out of the tunnel at Wembley – a brief moment of enclosed stillness and then...wow.

The coils of Sa Calobra suddenly reveal themselves beneath you as if you're perched at the top of a rollercoaster. The road twists and dives in and out of sight, seeming to pierce right through cliffs of white limestone, all framed by the blue of the Mediterranean. A pause for photographs – everyone does – and then you tilt over the edge to let gravity pull you into its embrace.

First, you swing through the 270-degree loop of the Nus de sa Corbata – literally, the tie knot – which throws you into a set of tightly stacked switchbacks. Now the road goes freeform, jinking and writhing like Maradona evading defenders. More switchbacks lead to a long section of lazy curves through hillsides strewn with boulders and stumpy pine trees. At one point, the road squeezes through a natural archway of rock that looks like it would crush any of the tourist buses that lumber up and down the slope every day.

Eventually, after nearly 10km (6 miles) of exhilaration, the road flattens out and the thrill ride comes to an end as you arrive at the seafront in Port de Sa Calobra, while the child's voice in your head keeps yelling, 'Again! Again!'

The harbourside is a pleasant place to while away some time, drinking more coffee, maybe even exploring some coves, while you contemplate the climb back up to Coll dels Reis. There is no chance to avoid it, because the climb is the only way out, unless you hitch a ride with one of the tourist buses or swim for it.

Fortunately, the ascent is not too punishing. The average gradient of around 7% is fairly consistent, allowing you to get into a rhythm that could be maintained for the whole distance were it not for the fact that you'll likely keep stopping to take photos. The journey back up allows more time to appreciate the surroundings in a way that isn't possible on the descent because you're too busy grinning and whooping.

What becomes obvious is that, pretty as Port de Sa Calobra is, it is not the reason that so many tourists visit this area. Everyone is here for the road, whether they are on four wheels or two, so if there is a downside to riding Sa Calobra, it is simply that it is >>

No other road on the planet can match the joyous swoops and swirls or playful loops of Sa Calobra

>> so popular. On a sunny weekend in summer you can expect to be sharing the space with a long string of cars, tourist buses, walkers, inline skaters and, of course, cyclists.

Strava is bulging with Sa Calobra's cycling ascents, and on a busy day it looks from above like colourful ants swarming over a nest. Mallorca is such a magnet for cyclists that every cafe on the island resembles an explosion in a Lycra factory, and everyone who comes here has to do Sa Calobra. Some will come here only to do Sa Calobra. Luckily, Mallorca has a climate that allows for year-round riding, so it's still possible to enjoy the exquisite curves of Parietti's masterpiece in splendid isolation if you choose your date wisely.

The final kilometre of the climb, where the gradient gets to around 9% or 10%, is the toughest. This is where thoughts turn from admiring the views to securing a decent placement on the Strava leaderboard.

Passing under the archway of the tie knot, the ever-present gaggle of cyclists lounging at the cafe will provide the impetus to push a little harder. You slingshot around the 270-degree loop and then it's an uphill sprint for 500m (1/3 mile) to get to the summit sign at Coll dels Reis.

After catching your breath, the obvious next step is to freewheel gently down to the junction with the Ma-10 main road again, perhaps stopping for another coffee at the Cafe Escorca if you have time. But before you do that, it's hard to resist backtracking for a couple of hundred metres, just for one more chance to lean over the Armco and gaze down once again at perhaps the most beautiful road ever built.

Summit height: 2,359m *(7,739ft)*
Altitude gain: 2,090m *(6,857ft)*
Length: 49.5km *(31 miles)*
Average gradient: 4.2%
Maximum gradient: 13%

Teide

There are many ways to ride up the big volcano on the small island of Tenerife. This is the most spectacular.

To say that Teide is on the island of Tenerife is perhaps a misnomer. Teide *is* the island of Tenerife – a massive volcano that rose out of the sea a few million years ago, and which is still active today. With a summit at 3,715m (12,188ft), it's the highest point in Spain, and no matter where you stand on Tenerife, if you face inland you'll be looking up at the third-highest volcano in the world (measured from the ocean floor, as they are).

That's assuming you can see the mountain at all. Being so big, Teide generates its own climate, so is often obscured by a ring of cloud. For the tourists enjoying a pint of Stella in one of the many traditional English pubs along the coastline, Teide is merely a hazy apparition in the far distance. If you want to unlock its secrets, you have to get up close and personal.

There are numerous ways to ascend Teide. From the northwest corner of the island, starting from Buenavista del Norte, you can pass through the magnificent Masca Gorge before taking the zigzag road that traverses up the western flank of the mountain in long, lazy sweeps. From the north in Puerto de la Cruz, the TF-21 road carves through forests of pine to emerge suddenly right at the lip of the volcano's caldera.

Perhaps the most popular route is from the south, starting from Los Cristianos, which provides a steep, writhing ascent that is a favourite test piece of the many professional cyclists who flock here for a bit of early-season altitude training.

It's little wonder that Tenerife is a favourite destination as a training camp. Being on the same latitude as the Sahara Desert, it has year-round sunshine; the high altitude is perfect for generating those valuable red blood cells that carry oxygen to our working muscles; and the roads are generally excellent (although it's also true that you will have to share them with the occasional tourist bus). Tenerife was where Ineos Grenadiers headed to prepare for their 2021 Tour de France campaign…but don't let that put you off.

This route tackles Teide from the east. The long, rambling ascent starts by heading north from the town of Güímar to get up onto the shoulder of the mountain, then makes a left turn to follow the ridge in a relatively straight line all the way to the top. >>

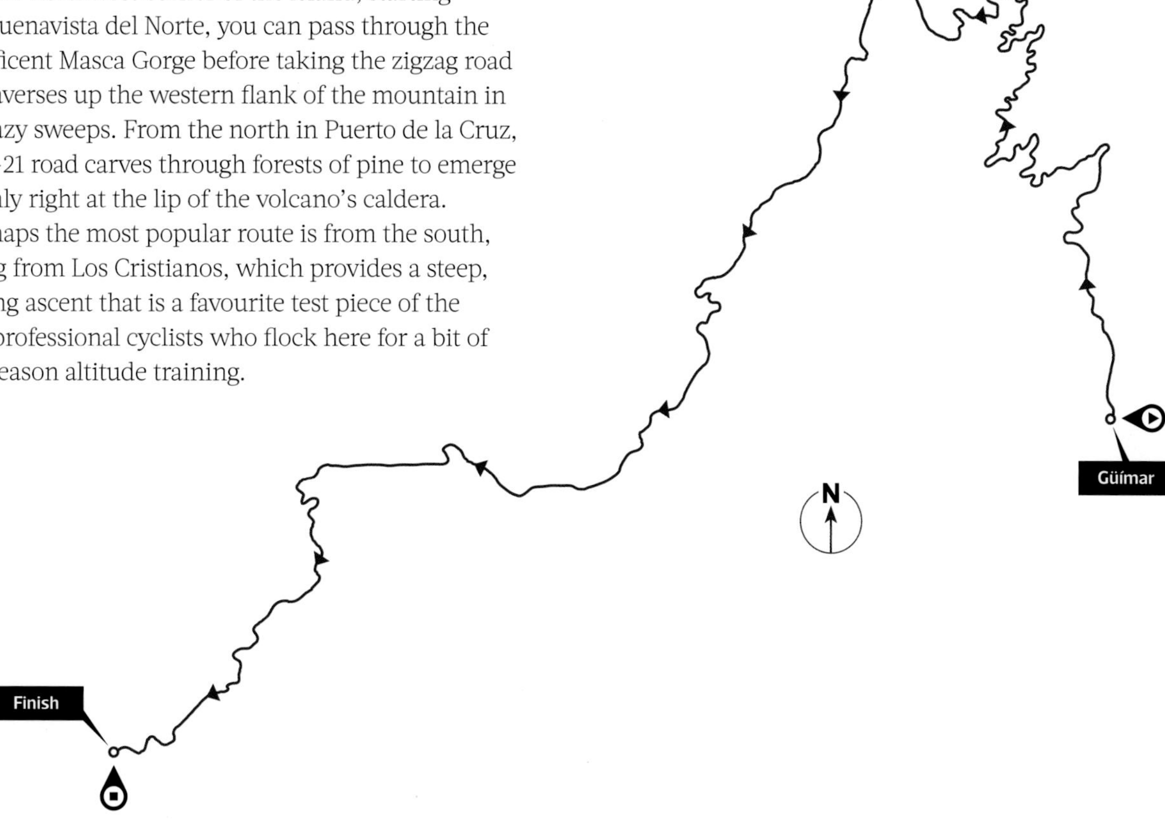

>> What makes it special is that much of the route is up above the treeline, allowing for spectacular views down to the coast, with the cone of Teide's summit frequently in sight, yet strangely somehow always just out of reach.

It's not strictly necessary to begin your ascent from the town of Güímar – but if you're skirting around the south of the island on the TF-28 then Güímar is where the road starts to head upwards towards Teide. The town itself is a jumble of blocky houses and narrow streets that give way to scrubby fields dotted with whitewashed hotels and brightly coloured homes. Once beyond the small town of Arafo, it becomes clear that you're gaining some serious height, even if it feels like the climb hasn't really started yet.

Now might be a good time to stop for a coffee, such as at the La Cueva de Nemesio a couple of clicks beyond Arafo. Sure, it's quite soon to be taking a break but beyond this point the opportunities for refreshment are increasingly scarce, and the temperature at this altitude is most likely pleasant for sitting on a terrace, which might not be the case in the kilometres to come. The TF-523 road meanders upwards at a reasonably consistent 4-5% gradient. The buildings disappear, but the views down towards the island's southeast coast become ever more expansive. That is, until you find yourself in thick woodland that obscures the vista but provides some welcome shade from the sun.

After climbing for 22km (13½ miles) from Güímar you finally arrive at the junction with the TF-24. If you turned right here you could enjoy a speedy descent to the island's capital at Santa Cruz de Tenerife. But you are turning left, to continue on the inexorable journey uphill, and you're not even halfway to the top yet. >>

Much of the route is above the treeline, allowing for spectacular views down to the coast

>> The trees continue to obstruct the view, but occasionally a gap appears, and through it is revealed the cone of Teide's summit, seemingly so far away as to be on another Canary Island altogether. The enormity of the climb now starts to dawn on you. And you also can't help noticing that it's beginning to get a bit chilly.

Tenerife, like many volcanic islands, generates its own microclimates such that it is possible to ride from beneath overcast skies, through damp fog, to emerge above the clouds in blazing sunshine and then end up riding past snow drifts, all in the same trip.

The landscape also changes from one kilometre to the next, starting with Mediterranean-style coastal towns, morphing into lush pine forests, and eventually becoming more arid, until all that's left is a barren moonscape of jagged, brown rocks strewn across empty lava fields.

The lunar feel of the surroundings is only heightened by the appearance after 34km (21 miles) of a series of domed observatory buildings, perched on a hillside and staring out into space. This marks a high point on the ride at 2,295m (7,529ft), but it isn't quite the end.

From the observatory, the road drops down for 6km (3¾ miles) – a welcome break for air-starved lungs – taking you into Teide's collapsed crater, before climbing again for a final 9km (5½ miles) or so, to reach the highest point on the ride at 2,359m (7,739ft).

It's hard to call it a summit, as it is essentially a giant bowl of dark dust and solidified lava, but at least there is no more altitude to gain. There is, however, more climbing to come to get back over the lip of the caldera. Then, the only decision to make is which of the many roads on offer you're going to take to get back down again.

2500
2000
1500
1000
500
0m
0km 5 10 15 20 25 30 35 40 45 49.5

Belgium

Summit height: 110m *(361ft)*
Altitude gain: 92m *(302ft)*
Length: 1,075m *(¾ mile)*
Average gradient: 9.3%
Maximum gradient: 19.8%

Muur van Geraardsbergen

The on-off darling of the Tour of Flanders, the Muur may be short, but it packs a lot of history into its 1,075m (3/4 mile).

You can't keep a good climb down. There was uproar when the Muur van Geraardsbergen (or Kapelmuur, or just the Muur – it goes by all three names) was removed from the Tour of Flanders in 2012. That year, the finish of the race was moved from Meerbeke, where it had been since 1973, to Oudenaarde, which meant that the classic pair of closing climbs, the Muur and Bosberg, were struck from the route.

In 2017, however, the race's start was also moved, from Bruges to Antwerp, which meant the MvG could once again be included in the race. Yet, sadly, it looked like the iconic incline had been neutered. The peloton would ascend it with fully 95km (59 miles) of the race still to run, making it too far from the finish to have any decisive impact on the outcome. It seemed that what was once a totem would now be just a token.

But when the 101st edition of the race rolled around on 2 April 2017, another legend of Flanders, Tom Boonen, had other ideas...

Climbing the Muur – which, encouragingly, means 'wall' – on a non-race day is a rather different experience. For a start, while the likes of Boonen attract hordes of cheering crowds behind barriers, it's unlikely that you will merit more than a glance from someone on their way to work or returning with the weekly shop, however lurid your jersey.

And while you might feel like you're attacking the bottom of the climb pretty aggressively as you go for a Strava time, you won't be able to hammer into it quite like the professionals do. They come tearing down between the shops on a straight descent along Oudenaardestraat and Grotestraat before crossing the river Dander and smashing into the first cobbles on Brugstraat.

After a rather dark start to the climb, you quickly emerge into the wide, open space of the market square with the impressive city hall on the far side. Should you be interested, there is the brother to the Brussels statue of the Manneken Pis (little pissing man) just to the left of the stairs.

There's no relief from the Muur just yet, however, as it's left in front of Saint Bartholomew's church and right in front of Remco Evenepoel's church (it's actually Bar Gidon with a banner from the young Belgian's fan club above the entrance, but it's appropriate given that he is likely to command a religious following among the locals in years to come).

The cobbles are barely worthy of the designation at this point, being nice and flat and wide with the gaps between generously filled. However, the gradient has >>

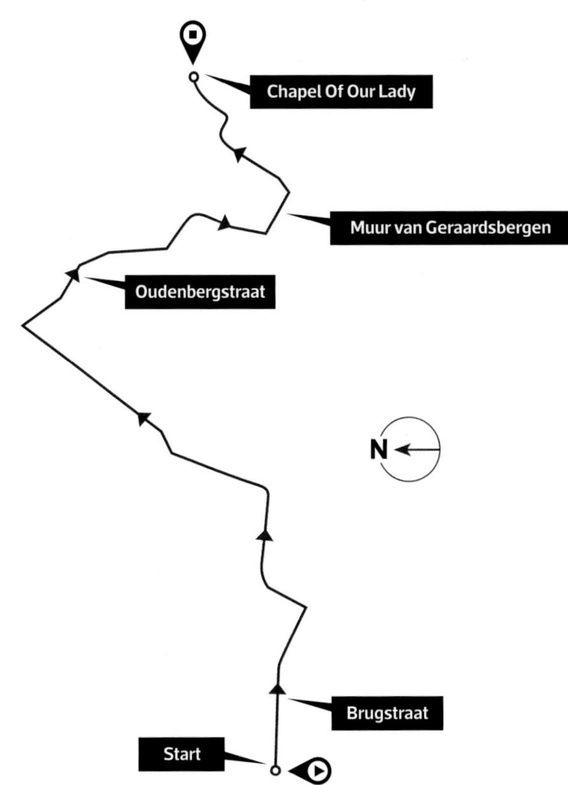

>> its first little dig into double digits as you ascend towards some fountains. Then, it's left onto the wide boulevard of Vesten with the neat townhouses on the right giving an excellent indication of the gradient. At the top you might be tempted to stop at the Cafe de Muur but you need to turn sharp right onto Oudenbergstraat. From here, it's a bit like following a river of cobbles back to its source as the wide street flows up past gardens and garages before narrowing into more of a trickling stream of stones when the climb enters the trees.

It was here, right at the crux of the climb in 2017, that Tom Boonen accelerated. He looked across at his QuickStep teammate, Philippe Gilbert, resplendent in the kit of the Belgian national champion, checked that he was ready and then laid down the watts. It doesn't look like much when you see it on television, but this narrow section, barely 100m (109yd) in length, is fearsome.

Suddenly, the gradient rears up to its maximum ferocity of 20% and the cobbles deteriorate to their juddering worst. If you haven't selected the correct gear before the left-hand bend at the bottom, you'll be in real trouble.

In just a few pedal strokes, the three-time winner of the Ronde, riding it for the last time, had exploded the race. Where there had been a cohesive bunch, now there was panic.

A group, including Gilbert, broke away from the main bunch, leaving the likes of Peter Sagan and Greg Van Avermaet floundering behind. Gilbert would eventually strike out for glory on his own with 55km (34 miles) to go and win solo.

Many will remember that 2017 race for Sagan crashing while chasing up the Oude Kwaremont (ironically at almost exactly the distance from the finish that the Muur used to reside), taking down Van Avermaet and Oliver Naesan in the process, but that wasn't the decisive moment. That had happened at a point much earlier in the race where no one thought it would or should, on the Muur. You can't keep a good climb down.

The denouement of the Kapelmuur is the famous curving climb to the *kapel* (chapel) itself. Perched atop a hill known as the Oudenberg, the Chapel of Our Lady with its red brick, grey slate and golden statue looks wonderfully neat, like a decoration set on a cake. The current neo-baroque building only dates back to 1906, but a hermit built a chapel here as long ago as 1294, although that was nearly 300 years after Geraardsbergen was established.

As you lean into the slope and head towards the wooden doors of the chapel, it will all seem very tranquil and quite the opposite of the roaring maelstrom that's televised on a race day, but that has its advantages. Tired though you may be by your 92m (302ft) of ascent, or perhaps keen as you may be to head on to the Bosberg, it's worth taking the time to have a peek inside the small chapel and then walk behind it to look at the view from the top of the hill.

The Kapelmuur might not have a spectacular vista such as those you will find at the summit of climbs in the Alps or Pyrenees, but it's still interesting. In fact, the Muur van Geraardsbergen arguably packs a greater variety, richer history and more intrigue into its single kilometre than many of the climbs found in the high mountains.

Mur de Huy

It may be only a fraction over 1km (2⁄3 mile) long, but the Mur de Huy in Belgium has crushed the will of many a cyclist – pro and amateur alike.

If you were writing a manual on how to win on the Mur de Huy at the end of La Flèche Wallonne – the Walloon Arrow – Spring Classic, you might scribble down three general rules. First, make sure you are among the leading ten riders through the climb's famous S-bend. Second, never make the first attack. Third, be Alejandro Valverde or Anna van der Breggen.

Okay, this won't be of much help to the non-pro hoping to tackle one of the most difficult climbs in Belgium. For mere mortals, it is simply hard from the start, then it gets harder and after that you're just hanging on to the point where even the flatter bit at the end feels like it's mocking you.

It's a climb that is so steep there really is no easy way up it. A long Alpine climb can often be tackled in a gear that allows you to spin and just take your time. The Mur de Huy, however, is simply too steep for any gear to be easy. >>

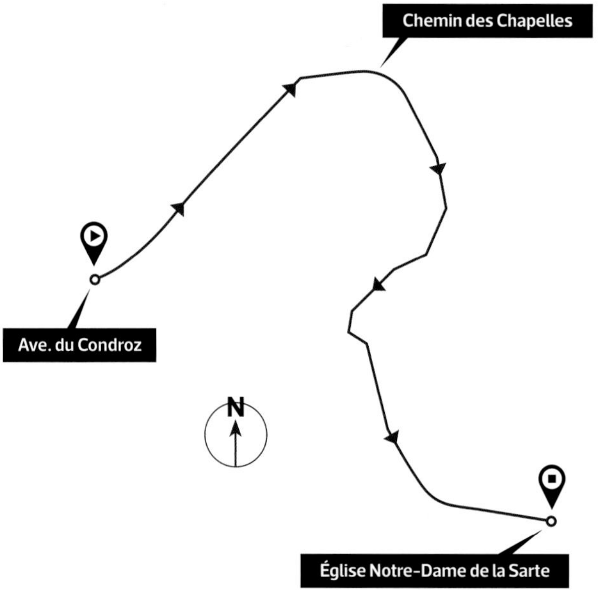

Summit height: 148m *(486ft)*
Altitude gain: 121m *(397ft)*
Length: 1,240m *(¾ mile)*
Average gradient: 10%
Maximum gradient: 25%

>> **Although the pros start climbing from the** centre of Huy, the real test begins as you turn off the Place St-Denis and onto the Chemin des Chapelles. The name of the road translates as the 'way of the chapels' and indeed there are six of them, ending with the church of Notre-Dame de la Sarte at the top. Since the 17th century there has been a festival once every seven years during which a statue of the Virgin Mary is taken from the church down to the town, via the chapels, where it is venerated for nine days.

At the bottom of this 900-m (984-yd) pilgrimage, the gradient actually looks relatively mild, which makes the fact that it is at least 10% feel even tougher on the legs. Pretty houses line the sides of the narrow road, giving it a slightly claustrophobic feeling initially, as if you're starting an effort from which there is no escape. The first chapel is on the outside of the first corner and looks more like a large white porch. Don't worry if you miss it, because all the others look the same. As long as you've seen one, you've seen them all.

Next, there's a small chicane, but don't be fooled into thinking this is the famous S-bend – that lies another couple of hundred metres up the road and when you reach it you'll be in no doubt. The tarmac rears up viciously as the cooling towers of the Tihange nuclear power station emerge over the houses behind you. If you're on the inside of the left-hander the gradient is over 25%, so it's unlikely you'll clock the monument to Belgian former pro Claude Criquielion as you wrestle with your handlebars.

Criquielion won Flèche Wallonne in 1985, the first year the race finished on the Mur, and his victory was made even more special by the fact that he not only won solo but was wearing the World Champion's rainbow stripes. He won again in 1989, this time attacking and distancing breakaway compatriot Steven Rooks on the very corner where the monument to Criquielion now stands.

Chapel number three is on the outside of the next right-hander, which signals the start of a more arboreal portion of the climb. For a few brief metres the incline eases, but this only serves to exacerbate the rise of the road afterwards as it curves left past chapel number four. This is the stretch where someone is always tempted to hit out in a bid for glory, but the winner will invariably keep their powder dry.

Between 2014 and 2017 in the men's race, that winner was Valverde, who won the race a record five times, while van der Breggen won seven women's >>

>> editions in a row up until 2021. This sort of dominance has led some to label La Flèche Wallonne as too predictable, perhaps even the weakest in the Ardennes week that begins with the Amstel Gold Race and ends with Liège-Bastogne-Liège.

Certainly, the women's race has seen several winning streaks, with Fabiana Luperini and Nicole Cooke winning three times and Marianne Vos five, before van der Breggen took on the baton in 2015.

Valverde's first win actually came in 2006, a whole eight years before his second, and another Spaniard with a long career won on the Tour de France's only stage finish up the Mur in 2015. Joaquim Rodríguez, pursued tenaciously by Chris Froome, went against convention and held on after attacking with about 300m (328yd) to go.

Regardless of whether you're racing or simply enjoying some recreation, those last few hundred metres must be some of the most interminable in cycling. The gradient remains constantly in the mid-teens and it seems to get longer between each white-painted Huy on the road, the three-letter words looking like a staircase leading to the top.

At least if you're only climbing it for fun you can enjoy the slight slackening of the incline as you pass the sixth chapel and head for the finish line. However, if you're racing other riders or the clock, this 'easier' last 100m (109yd) brings its own torment. It's easy enough that you can change up a few gears if you're chasing seconds, but you know that will sustain a pain that your legs and lungs could do without.

Once you've crossed the line and rolled to a stop at the side of the road by the lime trees, you might just worry that the climb has taken as much of a mental toll as a physical one, because staring at you from over a hedge is a diplodocus. The fact that it's standing in front of a ferris wheel doesn't lend any more normality to the scene, but rest assured you're simply looking at some of the taller attractions in an amusement park.

To further confuse you and make you wonder if you have in fact battled up a mountain, there's also a cable car station at the top of the climb. Sadly, it was closed after an accident in 2012, but it rams home the point that while the Wall of Huy might be short, it is also very sharp. An appropriate end to an arrow.

150
120
90
60
30
0m
0km 0.2 0.4 0.6 0.8 1.0 1.24

HUY

Summit height: 72m *(236ft)*
Altitude gain: 62m *(203ft)*
Length: 409m *(1/3 mile)*
Average gradient: 13%
Maximum gradient: 22%

Koppenberg

What this famous Belgian cobbled climb lacks in length, it makes up for in punch.

Rather like a single chapter in a book, it might seem slightly wrong to consider the Koppenberg in isolation. It's probably the most famous Flemish cobbled climb, but other chapters such as the Paterberg, Taaienberg, Eikenberg, Oude Kwaremont and Kapelmuur are all needed to make up the full, fantastic story of the Ronde van Vlaanderen – the Tour of Flanders.

And yet, it's also fun to inspect and dissect the nuances of a single inclined stretch of cobbles, and this particular hill near Oudenaarde is somehow representative of all that's tough, yet tantalizingly attractive, about the climbs that captivate the cycling world each spring.

Curiously, despite its status, the Koppenberg has only been a part of the Tour of Flanders since the mid-1970s. It was apparently used as a training ground by locals for many years (presumably on the basis of 'train hard, race easy'), but it didn't make its first appearance in the race until 1976 after a local resident, Hubert Hoffman, alerted the organizers to its existence. One suspects that Hubert's name wasn't on many of the peloton's Christmas card lists in subsequent years.

Even if you know what's coming, even if you've ridden it before, you can't help but feel intimidated by the Koppenberg, or *Steengat* (stone road) as it's also known. The cobbles begin just before the climb, the bike instantly convulsing beneath you. You try to maintain control, try to remember to relax, try to keep a strong core, even though there's an empty feeling in the pit of your stomach. You know the best way to tackle it is to hit it at speed so you barrel between the curiously uniform, often redbrick architecture that makes up the village of Melden at the bottom of the hill.

And then you see it – the river of pale grey cobbles rising up in front of you through the fields. Narrow, steep and disappearing into a dark tunnel of trees, it looks like a trap. It's as though you are pedalling inexorably up the ghastly tongue of a monster simply so that its shadowy mouth can swallow you up.

Initially, the gradient isn't too bad but you can still feel the speed built up on the flat bleeding away. And as your pace peters out, so you stop skimming across the surface of the stones and the cobbles become >>

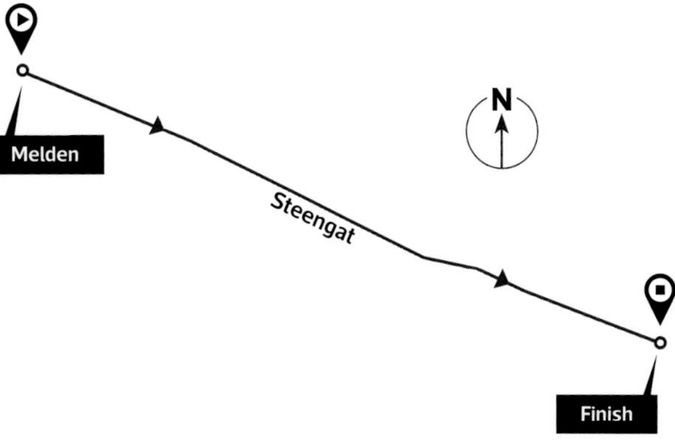

>> ever more exaggerated until your laboriously grinding tempo is such that each stone is a miniature mountain that your wheels must climb and descend in addition to the overall gradient.

Just before the banks rise up and the trees begin you might notice two fence posts on the right (you'll probably have other things to worry about, but they're there). This is where the cyclocross course escapes into the fields, but you don't have that option.

As you hit the hardest section and the incline spikes to over 20%, you're now committed to your choices. All your balance and strength is needed to stay upright and keep moving forwards, so if your hands are on the hoods that's where they are staying. Changing gear isn't an option either. Stop altogether and you will have to walk, which might seem preferable until you attempt the clawing, clattering combination of cleats and cobbles.

If you do have to stop pedalling, you won't be the first. The Koppenberg is rarely a decisive factor in producing the winner of the Tour of Flanders – it's too far from the finish and almost too difficult to allow anyone to make a difference – but it can nonetheless end the hopes of a large proportion of the peloton.

For riders not in the front group going into the climb, it is a lottery as to whether someone in front of them will wobble to a stop or touch a wheel and force everyone in the bottleneck behind to grind to a halt. Then, the race splits and those ahead continue up the road, never to be seen again.

Ironically, the most famous fall on this Flandrian hill was by a lone cyclist. Danish pro Jesper Skibby was on a solo break in 1987 when he stuttered, swerved and then toppled over on the steepest part of the climb. But it was what happened next that made the fall famous.

The driver of the commissaire who was following behind, seemingly more concerned about the proximity of the peloton than the welfare of the stricken Skibby, barged through in his BMW, crushing the back wheel of Skibby's bike in the process and only narrowly missing his feet. Boos bellowed out from the crowd on the bank – and no wonder, as it's still shocking to see on film today. The result was that the climb was deemed too dangerous and the race didn't come this way again for 15 years.

These days, the Koppenberg is a totemic part of the Tour of Flanders. Pushing on past the halfway point, you notice that, although the road is fairly straight, it's impossible to see the top. This is because the banks >>

Changing gear isn't an option. Stop altogether and you will have to walk

>> by the roadside are so steep, with their mass of hazel, birch and beech, that they hide the summit from view. But once between the banks, about where Skibby crashed, you see the light as though emerging from underground.

Battle on and the gradient eases as the trees thin. There's also a bench on the left that, as the view from it isn't worth the pause, seems to have been placed there purely to taunt you into stopping.

Thankfully, the cobbles are more tightly packed near the top and this allows a momentary touch of fluidity to your pedal strokes. Yet still you can't relax, because one last ramp remains to wring the remnants of resolve from your legs and lungs. Then, it's over. And as you haul the bike between the houses at the top, you can revel in the relief of a road that is flat and featureless.

In just two or three intense minutes it feels like you've experienced all the physical and emotional extremes of an hour-long mountain ascent. It's like a three-course meal compacted into a single pill. But the Koppenberg's 490m (1/3 mile) of riding and 62m (203ft) of ascent are anything but easy to swallow.

80
60
40
20
0m
0m 50 100 150 200 250 300 350 400 450 490

France

Luz Ardiden

In winter, Luz Ardiden is packed with skiers. In summer, this climb in the Pyrenees is often deserted – until the Tour de France comes to town.

Iban Mayo must have wondered exactly when the black cat crossed his path or where the ladder was that he'd walked under. Monday 21 July 2003 just wasn't his day. His legs were strong, he was riding high in the Tour de France and there was a contingent of Basque fans on the final climb of Stage 15 to cheer him on. But there was a fly in the ointment. At every pedal stroke, he was thwarted by a man wearing a yellow jersey...

That climb to Luz Ardiden begins, somewhat prosaically, at a mini-roundabout, the D12 spearing off the D921 to the west of Luz-Saint-Sauveur in the French Pyrenees. Immediately, you're into an ascent that will last just over 13km (8 miles) at an average gradient of 7.4%. Some large pipes provide the first landmarks, bisecting the road at right angles, presumably to service the town below.

For a climb with more hairpins than Alpe d'Huez, it seems odd that you don't really encounter any corners, let alone a switchback, until you're more than 2km (1¼ miles) into the climb. At 5% for that initial stretch, it's a relatively benign start in terms of gradient too, and although you're travelling through a tunnel of trees, it doesn't feel oppressive.

The village of Sazos provides a change of both scenery and gradient, throwing in four switchbacks in quick succession to make up for lost time. As you head the other way across the prevailing incline, you also get your first glimpses of a fabulous view. Below is Luz-Saint-Sauveur, cradled in the Pyrenean landscape. It's strange because in one glance the cluster of buildings looks safe and secure surrounded by snow-capped skyscrapers, but in the next glance the mountains seem to be menacingly overbearing. Of course, it's those same mountains from whence most people will have approached Luz Ardiden, as there lies the mighty Tourmalet.

Another kilometre through the trees and you reach the hamlet of Grust (of which more shortly), before a handful of hairpins leads you on to the toughest stretch of the whole climb. Averaging just over 9%, it's not the steepest gradient but it is sustained. In fact, what really characterizes the climb is its measured personality, which means you can get into a rhythm but also means you never really get a break.

The fact that the road was only built in the 1970s probably explains why it's pleasingly broad and why >>

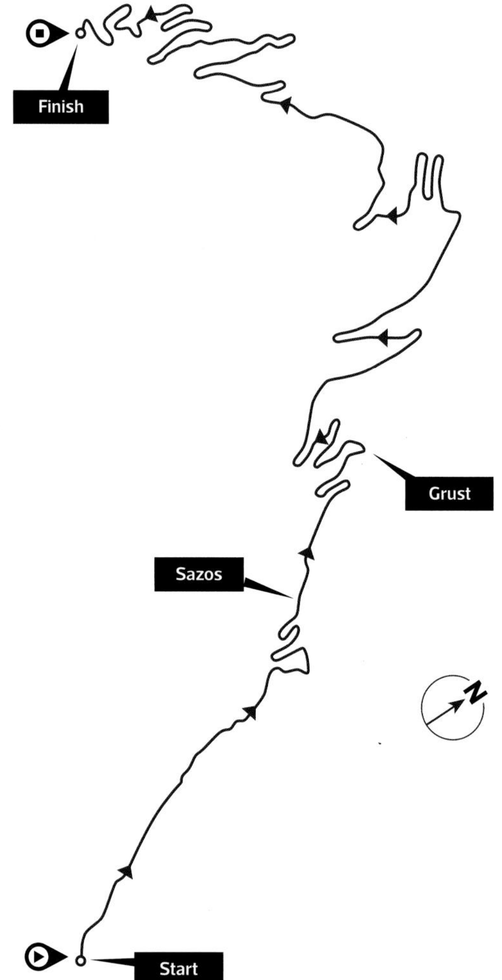

Summit height: 1,715m *(5,627ft)*
Altitude gain: 982m *(3,222ft)*
Length: 13.3km *(8¼ miles)*
Average gradient: 7.4%
Maximum gradient: 10.3%

>> the gradient is so regular compared to wilder, older roads up into the mountains. It also means Luz Ardiden is a relative newcomer to the Tour de France (and Vuelta a España), but it has certainly had its share of drama.

The coolest images must be of Greg LeMond in 1990. With his Z-team World Champion's jersey, Oakleys and no helmet, he looked the epitome of cycling chic. He didn't win that day – he merely set up his overall victory days later in Paris. Instead, he towed another iconic name to the top. Miguel Induráin, freed from Delgado domestique duties (Pedro was having a bad day, having won on the climb on its debut in 1985), stole the stage and established the natural order of things for the next five years.

But the most famous incident on Luz Ardiden? That brings us back to Iban Mayo. The man in yellow, you won't be surprised to hear, was Lance Armstrong. But he had only a slender lead over 1997 winner Jan Ullrich and hadn't looked anything like the dominant force of previous years. There was seemingly no attack in Armstrong. Early on the slopes of Luz Ardiden, Mayo stood on the pedals and opened a gap. But Armstrong followed, went to the front and slowly Ullrich reeled them back in.

Then it happened. Just before Grust, the careless Armstrong, riding too close to the crowd, caught his handlebars on a young spectator's bag. The American went down in an instant. Mayo had nowhere to go but into Armstrong, so found himself chewing the tarmac too. Mayo was up quicker and on his way, with Armstrong, full of adrenaline, setting off in pursuit soon after. He found Mayo's wheel once more, overtook and then his foot slipped off the pedal. He was launched onto the top tube and nearly took Mayo out again.

At this point, just up the road, Ullrich was soft pedalling, waiting in accordance with the peloton's >>

This relative newcomer to the Tour de France has certainly had its share of drama

>> unwritten agreement not to attack a leader who has been involved in a crash. Mayo and Armstrong managed to rejoin the group and for a while the status quo resumed, but then Mayo attacked again. Surely this time he'd get away? Except that once more Armstrong used the Spaniard as a springboard and this time Mayo could only stay with the American briefly before being distanced.

After the stage, Armstrong would say, 'Sometimes the best way for me to ride is angry, but I wasn't angry today when I attacked. I was a little bit desperate.' He was desperate because he knew he needed to put time into Ullrich before the final time-trial. Whatever it was that fuelled his attack, he dropped Mayo for good and forged on alone to win the stage.

Back on the road, a long left-hand bend takes you round the shoulder of the mountain and into the finishing amphitheatre. This is the spectacular slice of scenery that draws people to the climb.

The final 4km (2½ miles) snakes back and forth in a great grassy alcove. Ignore the right turn off the hairpin with just under 2km (1¼ miles) to go, watch out for the cattle grid 600m (656yd) later and then give it your all through the twists and turns of the final 750m (820yd).

At the top, it's obvious why it's such a quiet climb. There's nothing here in summer, apart from a rather retro building emblazoned with the ski resort's name. Mayo eventually sprinted past Ullrich for second place in 2003, but he was some 40 seconds behind Armstrong, who hadn't even been able to muster the energy to raise his arms as he crossed the line.

Once you've regained your strength, you'll be able not only to savour the view but also to look forward to a great encore. The broad, well-surfaced and relatively even climb also makes for a great descent.

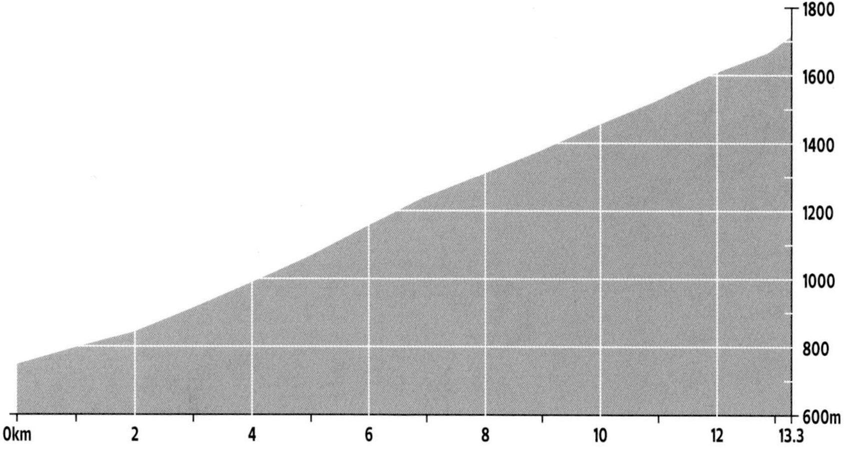

Col de la Madone

Tucked away near Nice on the French Riviera, this was the preferred test-piece of a certain Texan who didn't win the Tour de France seven times.

It might be a universally recognized distance, such as three kilometres or ten miles. Or it might be something more personal or arbitrary – to the end of the road and back, or the 19.5km to your parents' house that you always tell yourself is 20km away. Whatever it is, after a while, anyone who rides a bike usually starts testing themselves against a benchmark. We just seem to have this in-built desire to see how we measure up to some sort of set criterion. It's why Strava is such a success.

The Col de la Madone de Gorbio (generally known just as the Madone) is perhaps the ultimate climbing benchmark in cycling. A few people will be furrowing their brows at that and muttering something like 'Alpe d'Huez' or 'Ventoux', but the Madone is special.

For a start, unlike other classic climbs you could name, the Madone has never been used as part of a >>

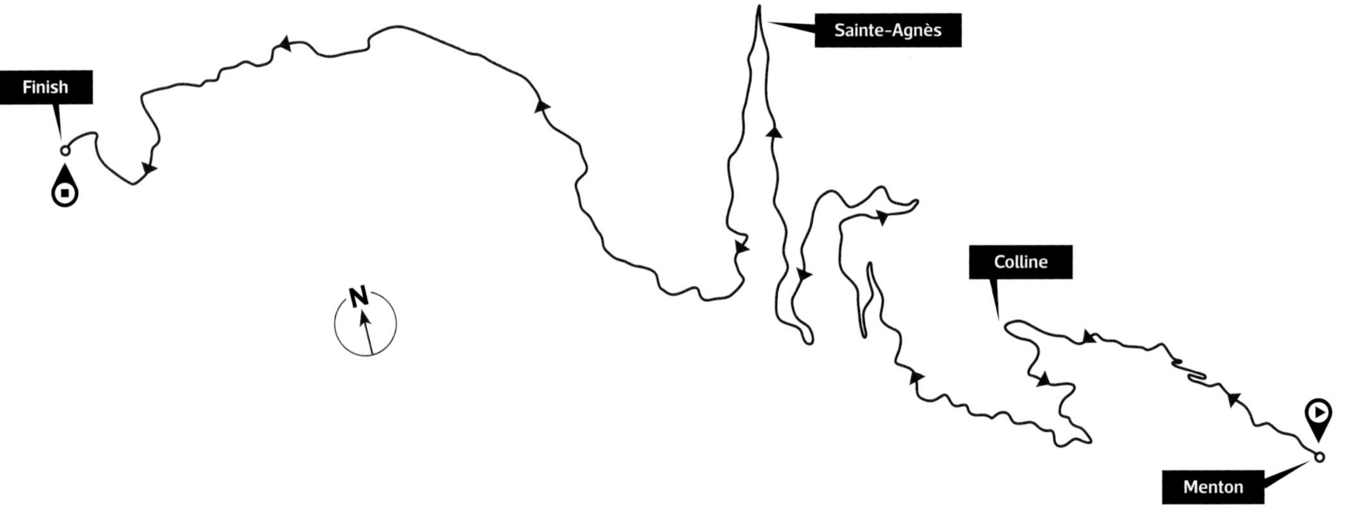

Summit height: 905m *(2,969ft)*
Altitude gain: 853m *(2,799ft)*
Length: 12.95km *(8 miles)*
Average gradient: 6.7%
Maximum gradient: 9.2%

>> Grand Tour. That means there is no particular section where a rider once famously put in an attack to break away for victory, there are no grainy photos of Coppi or Bartali, no videos on YouTube with Sherwen and Liggett's voices extolling riders' efforts. It's simply famous as a benchmark.

It's also not like a time-trial course, as it doesn't have a precisely defined length. There's a clear finish at the top, obviously, but where the climb actually starts is a matter of considerable debate. There are numerous competing Strava segments that start at different points, but its use as a test predates the social-competitive network and no one is quite sure which current GPS-defined start point was used in the past. Did Armstrong start at that particular sign? Did Rominger begin at that bus stop? To some, that

might be frustrating, yet the uncertainty adds to the alluring mystique.

Perhaps the best place to get going is the beach in the town of Menton, about 25km (15½ miles) along the coast from Nice. Starting at sea level somehow just feels appropriate, plus you can admire the mahogany tans and the Med over an espresso (it's right on the border with Italy, so the coffee is acceptable) before stretching your legs.

The climb follows the D22 and as you pedal through town, tackling traffic and roundabouts, you can see why the timed efforts tend to begin further on. Many of the potential starting points, including this ascent, are around the supermarket in Castagnins as it's just after here that the road narrows and loses its white line down the middle. Climb through a couple of hairpins and you'll see the huge concrete stilts of the A8 motorway towering over you, making you feel like an Ewok gazing up through the legs of an AT-AT Walker.

You loop round and go back under the motorway again, this time slightly closer to its grey underbelly, before turning back and heading over it as it tunnels unseen through the hillside beneath you. From here, more traditional views start to emerge of the mountains ahead and the sea behind. The houses on either side of the road begin to decrease in number, too, although there remain intriguing residential gateways at random intervals and you still feel relatively close to civilization at this point.

Traffic is typically thinner up here, although the wealth in this region means that when you do see a car there's a chance it might be a Ferrari. Of course, when Lance Armstrong was testing himself on these roads before the Tour de France, he might well have had a different Ferrari (Dr Michele) waiting for him at the top. Armstrong is perhaps the reason that this climb has such wide recognition, as he writes about it in *It's Not About the Bike*. He was also the one who suggested Trek name a bike after the climb.

How on earth do the pros make it up here in just half an hour?

The Madone's gradient is pretty steady, and although there's the odd brief spike it never strays too far from its 6.7% average. You can understand why it's such a popular test, because you don't have that fear of needing to leave something in reserve for a particularly hard pitch. You can just concentrate on steadily emptying the tank over the 13km (8 miles).

With a little over 5km (3 miles) to go to the top the road opens out into a slightly confusing expanse of >>

>> tarmac, with three roads spurring off it. This is Sainte-Agnès. The road you want is the small one (still the D22) that hairpins back immediately on your left.

From here, the character of the climb changes almost instantly, feeling much more remote and wild. The rock face remains on your right pretty much all the way to the summit and it has the ossified grey-white pallor of years bleaching in the sun. The road surface is rougher too, with patches of loose gravel. But with no barriers you're initially treated to a wonderful, unfettered view of the sea far below. It's nice to see how much altitude you've gained (your computer will tell you it's over 600m/1,968ft), but if you're testing yourself you won't have the energy for more than a glance.

There's some brief respite in the form of a flat half-kilometre (1/3 mile) that heads through the cool of two short tunnels, where you can gather your thoughts before the final push to the summit.

If you haven't ridden the climb before, it's hard to judge quite how near the top you are, as there's no obvious peak to aim for. The key is that when you go round a right-hander and find trees have returned, you can give it everything, because you're nearly there. Several plaques and the abandoned shells of various buildings mark both the top of the climb and the battles that took place here in the Second World War.

And, as you collapse over the handlebars feeling as empty as the buildings, you'll inevitably compare your own effort to the benchmark times of others. The numbers are likely to be sobering. How on earth do the pros make it up here in just half an hour?

Alpe d'Huez

Perhaps the most famous climb in professional cycling, every one of Alpe d'Huez's 21 hairpins has a story to tell.

The madness, the shouting, the speed of the cyclists as they head towards Alpe d'Huez...yes, the Megavalanche is quite an event. Of course, the same can be said for the Tour de France – it's just that road cyclists climb to the ski town from the valley instead of descending to it from the beautiful Sarenne Glacier like the mountain bikers at the annual mass-participation Megavalanche race. Alpe d'Huez is something of a cycling mecca whichever tribe you belong to.

The depart is less grand for a road cyclist than it is for a mountain biker, regardless of which start point you choose. When times were first recorded up through the 21 hairpins, the clock started at the roundabout on the D1091, but these days the official 'Chrono' sign stands 700m (766yd) further up the road. The reason? You actually descend slightly for that stretch, so it seems more appropriate to begin where the road tilts upwards.

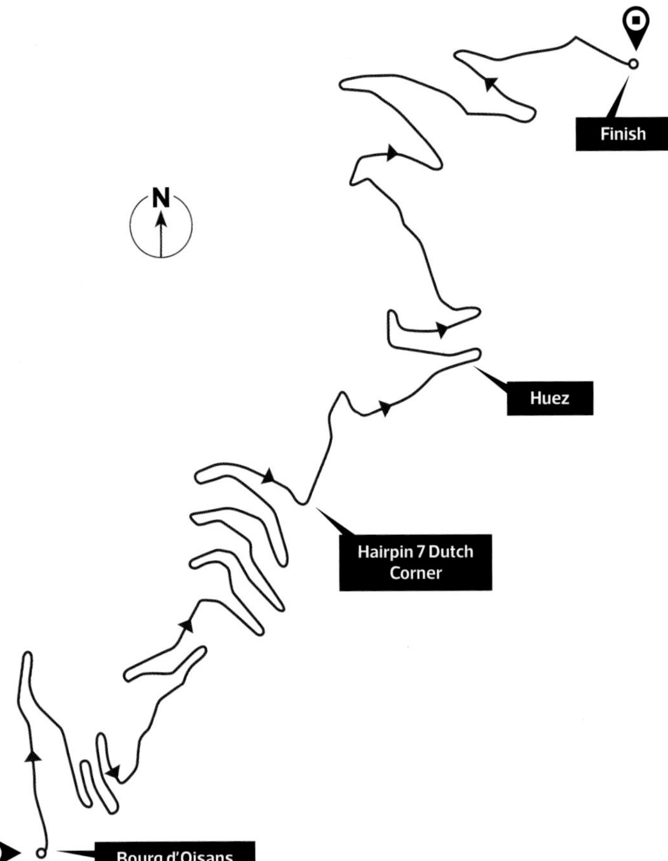

The temptation is to set off with leg guns blazing, but you'd be well advised to temper your enthusiasm, because at an average of 10% the first 2km (1¼ miles) are the most demanding part of the 13-km (8-mile) climb, and it's easy to use too much energy too early. The road is wide and well surfaced, and you hit the first hairpin after 700m (766yd). This is hairpin number 21, and you can begin the countdown to hairpin 1 at the top.

Each switchback is marked with a sign that, along with its number, includes the names of riders, in order, who have won on Alpe d'Huez. The first sign is arguably the most notable as it displays the names of Fausto Coppi (the first winner in 1952) and Lance Armstrong (the 22nd winner).

Although far from unpleasant, Alpe d'Huez is also far from being the most spectacular or technically interesting climb. The view across Bourg d'Oisans down in the valley to the mountains beyond is attractive without taking your breath away. You tend to settle into a rhythm on the bike, looking forward to the slight breather afforded by the relatively regularly spaced hairpins. And while the riding isn't easy, it's not crazy hard either, with the mildly fluctuating gradient hovering around 8% or 9% after those first couple of kilometres.

Perhaps the most striking visual aspects of the climb are the imposing, sometimes overhanging rock faces that dominate hairpins 13 to 8. Yet, in the same way that a vast stadium can only really be appreciated when packed to the rafters with thousands of voices singing about chariots, so I suspect Alpe d'Huez >>

Summit height: 1,835m *(6,020ft)*
Altitude gain: 1,089m *(3,573ft)*
Length: 13.2km *(8¼ miles)*
Average gradient: 8%
Maximum gradient: 10.6%

>> gets much of its legendary character from the people who flock here to watch a race.

There is perhaps no better example of this than the famous Dutch Corner (hairpin 7) where a Dutch priest called Father Jaap Reuten famously rang the bells after each Dutch win on the Alpe (and there were many in the 1970s and '80s). For a few hours in July, this big bend becomes a broiling cauldron overflowing with orange bodies and smoke from flares, but during the rest of the summer the small church on the inside of this very open hairpin stands silent. Without the hordes of raucous tangerine fans, the corner is fairly nondescript.

Still, just as if you put Sir Ian McKellen and Dame Judi Dench on an unexceptional amateur stage and broadcast their performance to the world it would gain instant fame, so Alpe d'Huez has been elevated to the iconic by the exceptional performances that have played out on its slopes over the years.

Famous scenes include Greg LeMond and Bernard Hinault crossing the line arm in arm in 1986, after the Frenchman had been a dubious teammate to the American up the Alpe's slopes. Or Marco Pantani in full flight in the 1990s, when he set what many still believe to be the quickest time up the climb at 36min 40sec (this was, of course, back in the days before Strava). Or Giuseppe Guerini colliding with a spectator in 1999, but getting up to win the stage; 'the look' given by Armstrong to Jan Ullrich in 2001 after rope-a-doping him earlier in the stage; the less salubrious but nonetheless notorious allegation that Michel Pollentier tried to fool doping control in 1978 by giving a sample from a hidden pouch full of someone else's urine. All these took place on Alpe d'Huez.

Even without these tales, the Alpe would have a crucial place in the Tour's history. When a hotelier >>

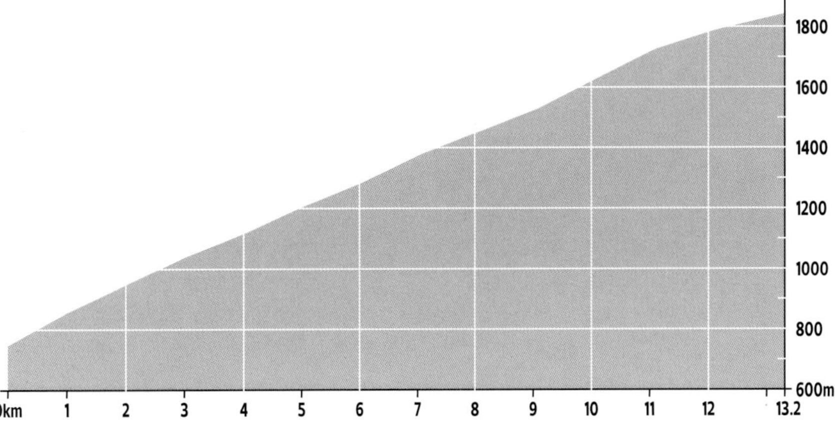

Alpe d'Huez has been elevated to the iconic by exceptional performances on its slopes

>> named Georges Rajon first managed to persuade the organizers to route the Tour up to the ski resort in 1952, Alpe d'Huez became the race's first ever summit finish. That same Tour was the first to be covered by motorcycle TV crews, so the Alpe's fame should have been guaranteed when the glamorous Coppi crossed the line. But, extraordinarily, Alpe d'Huez wasn't used again for a dozen years and then only as a mid-stage climb. Then, it had another 12-year hiatus until 1976, so Alpe d'Huez certainly wasn't an instant classic.

The finish of the climb seems to be a long time coming. Once you emerge from the trees into the village of Huez just above Dutch Corner, it feels like you must be nearly at the top, but it's a false summit.

The final four kilometres ($2\frac{1}{2}$ miles) stretch out through the upper meadows and you feel as though you're within touching distance of the resort for some time before you actually reach it. Then, all of a sudden, you round the final hairpin (with its sign honouring Giuseppe Guerini), scale the final ramp past some flats and you're at the finish line. If you go under the bridge, you've gone too far.

Despite its utilitarian ski resort appearance, the settlement of Alpe d'Huez is much older than it looks and it has a history of silver mining that goes back to medieval times. More recently, it was the first resort of its kind to install a ski lift.

But for all its other claims to fame, Alpe d'Huez will be inextricably linked to the Tour de France. So much has occurred here that this relatively modest 13.2-km ($8\frac{1}{4}$-mile) climb, which tops out well below 2,000m (6,562ft), has been elevated to stand alongside spectacular Grand Tour giants such as the Galibier, Tourmalet and Stelvio.

alpe huez
À chacun son virage !
PIC DE L'ALPE
VIRTU

Col Agnel

Straddling the border between France and Italy, steeped in history and soaring to a great height, the Col Agnel deserves more attention.

A bit like Chris Froome's Grand Tour potential before he hit the big time, the Col Agnel is underappreciated. After all, at 2,744m (9,003ft) it's the third-highest pass in Europe (and eighth-highest road), beaten only narrowly by the glamorous celebrity climbs of the Col de l'Iseran (2,770m/9,088ft) and Stelvio (2,750m/9,022ft).

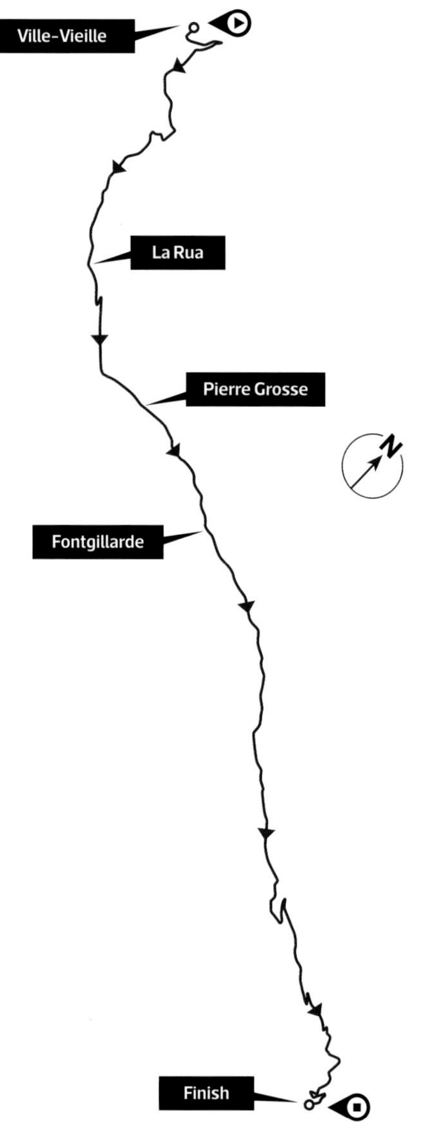

Straddling France and Italy, Agnel is also the highest border crossing in Europe. As a test of climbing chops, it's a decent 20.6km (12¾ miles) in length from Ville-Vieille on the French side and it averages a healthy 7%. The final 5km (3 miles) of the climb in the thin air above 2,200m (7,218ft) actually averages closer to 9%.

So, it's fair to say the numbers stack up in favour of fame. But, of course, it takes more than just the right numbers on paper for a climb to achieve stardom.

In the same way that a good VO2 max doesn't automatically mean you will be a Tour de France winner (you might have the mental fortitude of a damp lettuce leaf, for example), so an ascent needs more subjective attributes to commend it to the pantheon of great climbs. Attributes such as attractiveness, for example, are a help.

Here too the Col Agnel fits the bill. In any catwalk of climbs, this one would be up there in supermodel territory, unable to get out of bed for less than the price of an Ineos Grenadiers contract.

Admittedly, the first half of the climb isn't particularly spectacular, but it's also far from ugly once you're underway from the roundabout at Ville-Vieille where the D5 spears away from the main D947 and across the river Guil. You work your way up through trees for about 5km (3 miles) and then, just after the >>

>> landscape starts feeling a little more pastoral, you'll see the first of several tiny villages. This is La Rua, and almost immediately after it you need to dart off to the left, taking the D205 into the cluster of chalets that make up Molines-en-Queyras.

The hamlet of Pierre Grosse arrives next, then Fontgillarde. And while each bunch of buildings gives you something to aim for and provides bucolic scenes, such as a game of geriatric *boules*, to distract you, the road also seems to rise up steeply at some point through each one. Why villages often have these sharp ramps is open to debate, but they certainly don't provide much respite for the legs.

Once the final sloping roof of Fontgillarde has slipped past, you're in the truly beautiful part of the Agnel. Apart from the thin ribbon of tarmac, it feels as though civilization has ceased to exist. Traffic, which has never been more than a steady trickle up to the junction at Le Serre anyway, now just melts away. It's as if you've been gradually returning to nature ever since the beginning of the climb. From the shops at the start you pass through ever sleepier villages until everything man-made has evaporated and you're left only with the sounds of birds and babbling water, the occasional marmot or cow, and the wind.

Some climbs are like pedalling your way through a sort of cycling theme park. The graffiti on the road, the cafe at the top, the sense that you are following in the wheels of thousands of others that have gone before, the selfies, the commemorative jerseys on sale...none of this applies to the Col Agnel. It feels blissfully unadorned.

This third quarter of the climb, between the villages and the steep last 5km (3 miles), is itself rather unusual for an entirely different reason. Instead of snaking >>

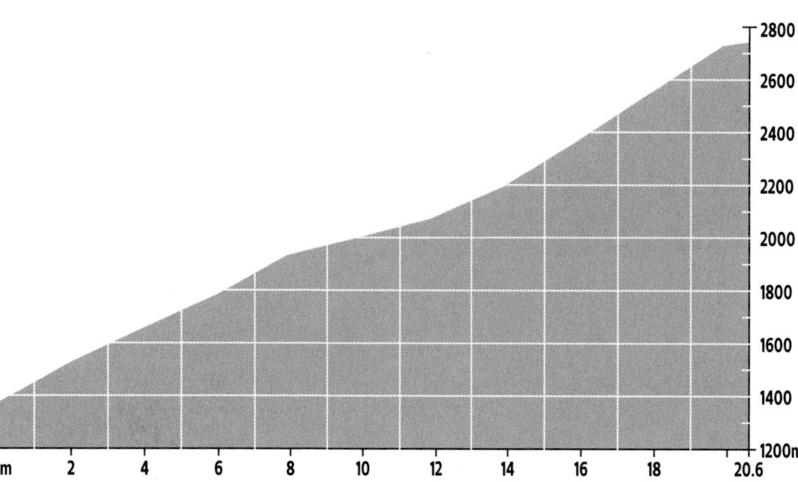

The wild, unspoilt nature of it is a part of what makes this climb not only beautiful, but special

>> back and forth across an incline, it plots a mildly meandering but essentially straight course up a valley. It's not even all uphill, with the occasional short descent and flat section thrown in as you pedal against the flow of the gin-clear stream to your right. The only problem is, if the wind is blowing directly down the valley, there isn't the usual fluctuating switchback feeling as you tack back and forth across a slope. You simply have to battle into it.

Talking of battling, you may now be following in the weighty footsteps of Hannibal's war elephants. While it's more likely his army went over the Col du Petit

Saint-Bernard or the Col de Clapier further north, the Agnel is a possible route, and it's a welcome distraction imagining what might have occurred here more than 2,000 years ago.

The Tour de France has rarely beaten its own path over the Agnel, and when it came in this direction on Stage 15 in 2008 it was a leg-softener, with the stage finishing up at Prato Nevoso. The Giro d'Italia is also an infrequent visitor from the Italian side, where it is known as the Colle dell'Agnello (the pass of the lamb). The Giro's visit in 2016 saw arguably the Agnel's most famous cycling moment to date, as Steven Kruijswijk crashed into a snow bank while descending, effectively ending his hopes of winning the race. A few moments earlier, Michele Scarponi had led over the summit, and there is a memorial to the late Eagle of Filottrano at the top of the pass.

The Agnel's anonymity is no doubt connected to its lack of Grand Tour action. But it verges on crazy that the third-highest pass in the Alps, one that lies so close to the Izoard and Galibier, has been used so little. Col Agnel deserves its place in the pantheon of classic climbs, and if you ever find yourself breathing hard in the thin air of its hairpinned finale you too will be in no doubt that it stands shoulder to shoulder with the very best.

Perhaps you will also come to another conclusion: that it's something of a blessing that the Agnel remains largely untrammelled by professional racing and is relatively unknown as a result. Because the wild, unspoilt nature of it is a large part of what makes this climb not only beautiful, but special. Maybe some things should remain underappreciated.

Summit height: 2,115m *(6,939ft)*
Altitude gain: 1,404m *(4,606ft)*
Length: 19km *(11¾ miles)*
Average gradient: 7.4%
Maximum gradient: 14%

Col du Tourmalet

It's the *hors catégorie* climb the Tour has visited more than any other. But that doesn't make it any easier.

'Crossed Tourmalet. Very good road. Perfectly feasible.' That's reportedly how Alphonse Steinès communicated his passage over the famous climb, after doing a recce for organizer Henri Desgrange ahead of its initial inclusion in the 1910 Tour de France.

Steinès was clearly the sort of person who liked to look on the bright side of life. He and the Black Knight from Monty Python would have got on famously.

'Only a flesh wound!'

'Merely a hillock!'

Steinès, you see, had indeed crossed the Tourmalet, but only just. Having abandoned the car and driver he had set out with, he then paid (with gold coins) a shepherd boy to guide him to the top. Despite the promise of more money if he reached the summit, conditions were so bad that the boy turned back.

Exhausted, stumbling, practically hypothermic having slipped into a stream and with warnings about bears ringing in his ears, Steinès was eventually found by a search party just before 3am. After no more than a restorative bath in Barèges, Steinès fired off the cheerful telegram to Desgrange.

The extent of his overly optimistic description duly became clear when Octave Lapize called the organizers 'murderers' during the first Tour stage to feature the Tourmalet (the monstrous 326-km/202-mile stage >>

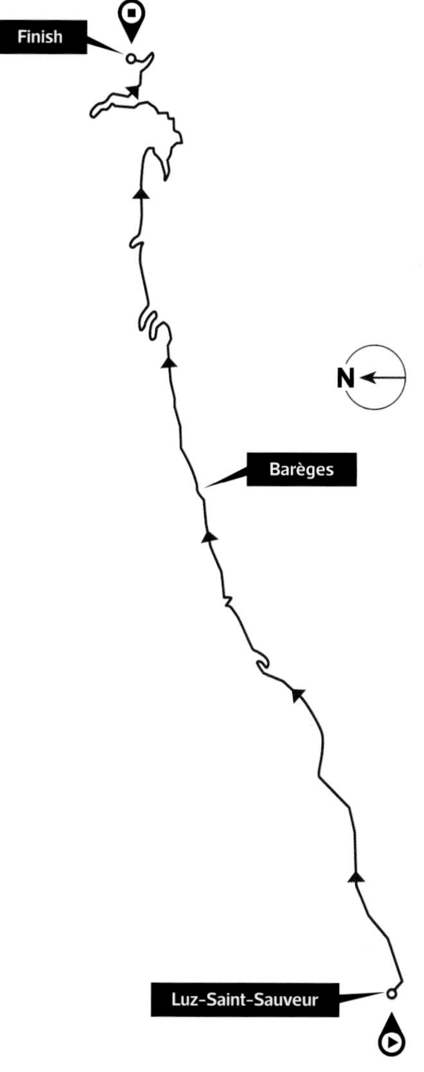

>> also featured the Aubisque, Peyresourde and Aspin).Given that Lapize won the stage and the Tour in 1910, who knows what the rest of the riders must have thought. Not that this discouraged the organizers of the Tour, because the Tourmalet has long been the most-used climb in the race.

This route tackles the climb from Luz-Saint-Sauveur in the west. Unusually for a *col* (a mountain pass), both sides are almost equally difficult. Climb this side and you travel 19km (11¾ miles) at an average gradient of 7.4%, while from Saint-Marie-De-Campan to the east (the direction from which Steinès and Lapize tackled it) you have 17.2km (10¾ miles) of climbing also at an average of 7.4%.

It's a climb of two halves, with the first part less spectacular but also more deceptive. It would actually be easy enough to skip straight to the more aesthetically pleasing second half, as there is an obvious and tempting starting point at a vast ski station car park. However, you need to have your legs softened up by the easier first half to understand the true difficulty of the Tourmalet.

As you climb from Luz-Saint-Sauveur, the road is meandering, with the rocky river Bastan sticking tight to the left of the tarmac. The occasional hairpin lulls you into thinking things are spicing up, but then the D918 settles back to its straight course up the valley, and this continues through Barèges and on to the car park over 10km (6¼ miles) into the climb.

What's deceptive about this first stretch is the gradient. The road isn't remarkably wide, but with a white line down the middle and plenty of room for two-way traffic it disguises the steepness well. Your eyes would swear it was only about a 4% incline, but your legs and bike computer will tell you that it's about twice that. >>

2200
2000
1800
1600
1400
1200
1000
800
600m
0km 2 4 6 8 10 12 14 16 18 19

>> Just before you reach the vast car park you may notice some small green-and-white signs with depictions of cyclists on them and arrows pointing right towards the Voie Laurent Fignon. This is the old road up the Tourmalet, which has been left in place for non-motorized traffic. The Tour sticks to the main road, but if you do have a desire to head up the old road just watch out for stones. The lighter traffic means the road isn't quite as well swept as the new tarmac, and punctures could be a problem.

Back on the D918, the wide road continues to a big right-hand hairpin where the gradient disappears for a few blissful pedal strokes. Enjoy the brief break, because the incline is unrelenting from here to the summit 5km (3 miles) away. Almost immediately after this corner the white line down the middle vanishes and the road seems a little wilder as a result.

You're now entering the craggy jaws of the mountain fortress that has been looming ahead of you for the whole ride. No serried stacks of switchbacks here, just a punishing path wriggling its way up the slopes.

As the road gets narrower you can feel quite exposed, with seemingly little or no protection from the drops at the side. A wobble here and you feel you'd be tumbling for some time. That's assuming you can see the side of the road. When the Tourmalet held a summit finish in 2010, a thick, swirling mist surrounded the riders almost as closely as the spectators did.

The 1.8km (1 mile) from the penultimate hairpin averages 11%, and as you round the last switchback with only 400m (1/4 mile) to go you're presented with a ramp that spikes up to over 14% in one final attempt to make you capitulate. By being forced to tackle the hardest pitch last, you really do feel as though the mountain is wringing the remaining drops of strength from your muscles.

The reward for making it all the way up, however, is a beautiful finish line. The way the road crests between two walls, with vast valleys in front and behind, feels like a true summit. And atop the left-hand wall, standing proud like a figurine on a wedding cake, is a silver-coloured sculpture of Octave Lapize straining with the sort of effort that does indeed look as though it might kill him.

Since 2001, the first person over the top in the Tour has been awarded the Souvenir Jacques Goddet, netting the rider a handsome bonus. You can pick up your own souvenir at the shop on the summit if you want, but just getting to the top feels like reward enough.

The French call the Col du Tourmalet '*l'incontournable*' (the unavoidable), because it's the only way across this part of the Pyrenees, which partially explains why the *col* has been used so many times in the Tour. But it really is only part of the reason, because it is also, as Steinès said, a very good road.

Col d'Izoard

Few climbs look like the Izoard or can match its place in Tour de France folklore. This is one in which to savour every metre of ascent.

Of all the climbs in this book, the Izoard has the most relaxing start. Clip in at the village of Guillestre and the Izoard greets you in a friendly fashion. Yes, there's a bit of traffic on the D947, but the road is wide and the air is often cool as the sun struggles to find a way down into the steep-sided gorge. The gradient is also more of a false flat, so you can easily turn the legs over with the chain on the big ring.

And as you pedal, quietly pleased at how quickly you're ticking off the 31.5km (19½ miles), it's worth thinking of Fausto Coppi. When he raced along here on the way to the summit in 1949, he'd started the day with the smell of the sea in his nostrils. It seems crazy now, but the stage had begun all the way down on the coast in Cannes, and this had been the norm since the Izoard first featured in the Tour in 1922. These days, any stage over the Izoard tends to start much further inland.

After 16km (10 miles) of relatively relaxed cycling, a couple of hairpins grab your attention and mark the end of the false flat. Soon, you need to turn left onto the D902, otherwise you're heading for the Col Agnel and the Italian border. This junction is really the start of the climb proper and, as if to ram the point home, there is a Tour de France sign, with the climb's statistics depicted on it.

The numbers reveal that from this point the ascent is 14.1km (8¾ miles) long with an average gradient of 7.3%, a maximum sustained gradient of 10% and a finish line at an altitude of 2,360m (7,743ft). But actually, the hard work only really starts in the >>

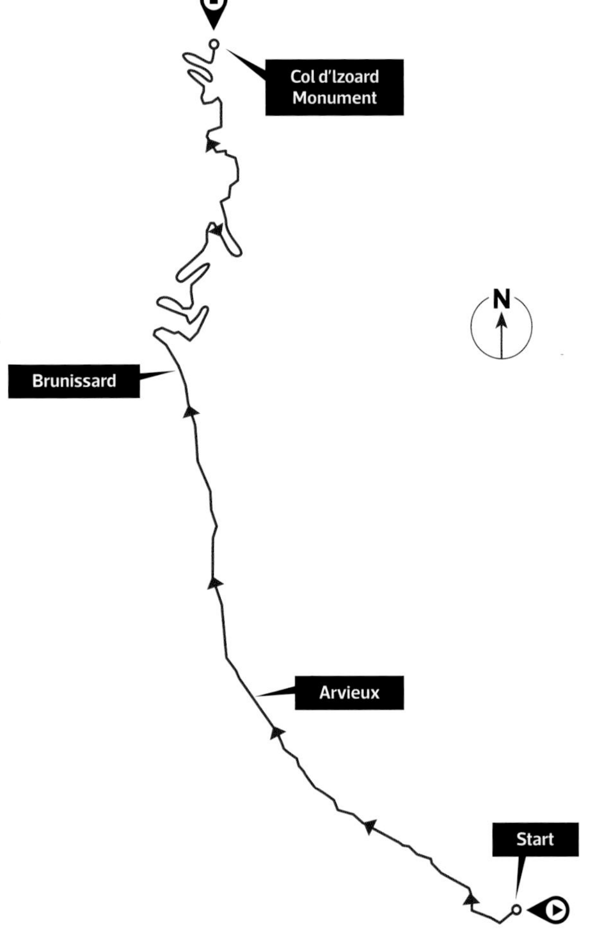

Summit height: 2,360m (7,743ft)
Altitude gain: 998m (3,274ft)
Length: 14.1km (8¾ miles)
Average gradient: 7.3%
Maximum gradient: 14%

Tunnel
de la Maison
du Roy

>> second half of this section of the climb. For the 7km (4¼ miles) from the last village to the top, the average gradient is more like 9% and there are a couple of kilometres that average more than 10%.

The D902 is narrow and it meanders before straightening as the valley blooms. It's usually hot too, with the sun on your back and no trees to shade you, although plenty of pines stand tantalizingly out of reach on the valley sides. Three small settlements give you something to aim for as you ride between great green meadows, but at times the road seems to be an even falser flat than that opening stretch.

The road's width and lack of corners disguises the 7–8% gradient horribly, wearing you down until it culminates in a final ramp out of Brunissard that doesn't look difficult but feels interminable as it flares up to 14%. Then, the first hairpin arrives and you crawl in among the trunks and the welcome shadows thrown by the evergreens. This is where the gradient consistently cranks up a couple of degrees more, and although the switchbacks provide some welcome targets to aim at, the respite they offer is fleeting.

Coppi wasn't alone when he climbed here in 1949; alongside him was his fierce rival Gino Bartali, the pair having dropped Ferdi Kübler after a flurry of punctures had thwarted him. It would be another puncture that would ensure the stage went down in history.

Coppi crested the Izoard first but Bartali was with him (the peloton 15 minutes in arrears by this point) and they descended together before, agonizingly, >>

>> Bartali punctured 10km (6¼ miles) from the finish in Briançon. Incredibly, Coppi waited for his rival and was duly beaten in the sprint for the stage victory.

Why? Perhaps it was because it was the 18th July and therefore Bartali's 35th birthday. Perhaps it was because both Coppi and Bartali knew that the younger man would be the one to go on and win the Tour overall that year. Either way, it was an act that seems almost bewildering in this day and age of competition.

Soon, you're in for a surprise – a descent. Going downhill in the middle of climbs can be disconcerting because, while pleasant, it can upset any rhythm that you might have settled into. Plus, you know that it's damaging that average gradient figure and making the climb look easier to the outside world than it really is. The bonus in this case is that you can claim to have bagged two *cols* for the price of one, as technically the first 30km (18½ miles) or so of climbing is up the Col de la Plâtrière, with the Col d'Izoard taking the glory for the last 2km (1¼ miles) to the summit.

But it's the bottom of the brief descent and the start of those kilometres to the summit that scenically sets the Izoard on a pedestal. The huge pale scree slopes and scattered spikes of stone are known as the Casse Déserte, and it's a landscape that is somehow both barren and beautiful.

This is where Louison Bobet's wife would be waiting to cheer him on, while his father waited on the hairpins above with a restorative sponge. Bobet was first over the Izoard on no fewer than three occasions during the Tour in the 1950s, and it is his face that you will see, alongside Coppi's, set into a rock face to the left of the road just at the end of the Casse Déserte.

In fact, given the choice, I would actually shun any tilts at the Strava segment and pause here, rather than at the very top. The last 2km (1¼ miles) are beautiful, with stunning views back down the valley, but the summit car park itself only has a slender stone tower (and a place that looks like the entrance to an old swimming pool). There's really nothing up top to rival the Casse Déserte's more rugged monuments to Bartali and the elegant Frenchman who was the first man to win the Tour three times in three consecutive years.

So before you tackle the final handful of hairpins to the summit, pause down here, admire the view and catch your breath. You don't have to stop for long – about the amount of time it would have taken Bartali to mend that puncture should be enough.

2400
2200
2000
1800
1600
1400
1200m
0km 1 2 3 4 5 6 7 8 9 10 11 12 13 14.1

Summit height: 2,802m *(9,193ft)*
Altitude gain: 1,586m *(5,203ft)*
Length: 23.2km *(14½ miles)*
Average gradient: 6.6%
Maximum gradient: 16%

Cime de la Bonette

Is it Europe's highest pass or isn't it? You'll have plenty of time to decide as you ascend the mighty Bonette.

Sometimes a start is hard to find. Particularly that sneaky start to a Strava segment. But climb the Route de la Bonette from the north and the start is simply the point at which you turn off the D900 and cross the wide Ubaye river in the small town of Jausiers. From here, you have around 22km (13½ miles) of riding to the top of Europe's highest pass...according to the signs.

Except you don't, because Europe's highest pass is the 2,770m (9,088ft) high Col de l'Iseran, about 200km (124 miles) away. It's all a bit complicated, but to reach the start of the Bonette's descent to Nice you only have to climb to 2,715m (8,907ft). If you want to, however, you can climb on up round an extra loop to 2,802m (9,193ft), which is the highest piece of tarmac in France (the highest in Europe being the Veleta in southern Spain at 3,398m/11,148ft). What's more, the signs can't decide whether this is the Route de la Bonette or the Route de la Bonette-Restefond.

To be honest, none of it matters. All you really need to know is that this is a climb that should be on your 'to do' list, because it's absolutely stunning. You go from valley to valley and feel as though you're on a journey through the mountains. You seem to climb in and out of four or five separate sections, each with its own flurry of hairpins, each different in character. >>

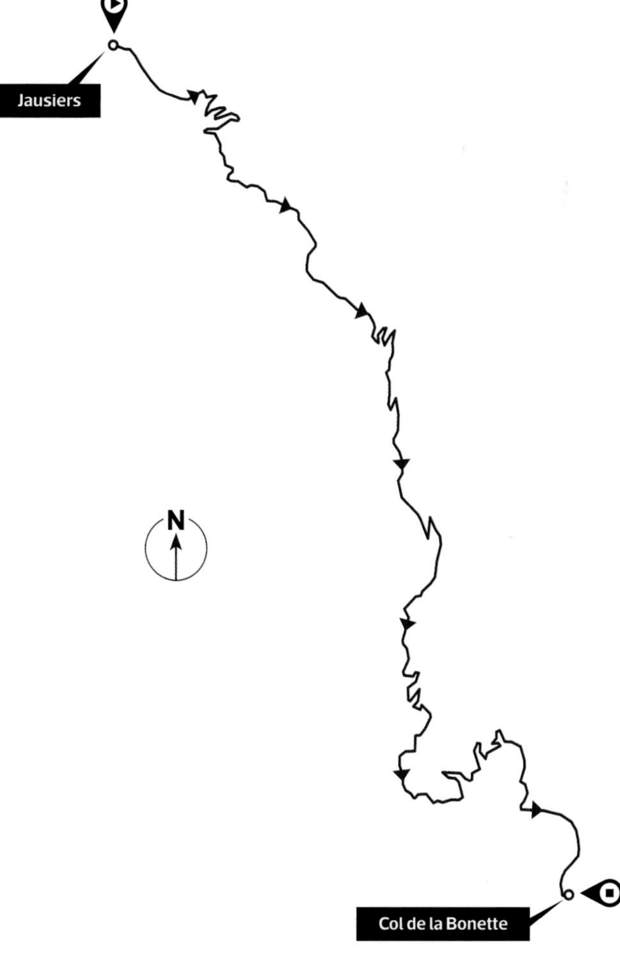

>> The road is narrow, with no white lines down the middle and no graffiti on the tarmac. This gives the climb a feeling of intimacy despite the grand scale of the scenery. The gradient averages a relatively friendly 6.6%, and although the incline spikes up to double figures it only does so in brief, manageable chunks. It's not easy, but it doesn't feel impossible either.

Considering that the Tour de France organizers love headline-grabbing altitudes and a nice drop of scenery to splash on the telly, it seems crazy that the Bonette makes only rare appearances in the race. The Souvenir Henri Desgrange (the prize for the first rider up the Tour's highest climb) is obviously awarded on the Bonette whenever it features, but it can't claim a summit finish because there's barely room to swing your arms, let alone park the Tour circus. But despite its rarity in races, the Bonette's stature as a climb is cemented by the man who crested it first in both 1962 and 1964.

Federico Bahamontes, The Eagle of Toledo, won the King of the Mountains classification in all three Grand Tours. In fact, he won it no fewer than six times on the Tour as well as taking the overall victory in 1959. In 2013, during the 100th edition of the Tour, Bahamontes was declared the best climber in the history of the race. The fact that the French awarded him the title ahead >>

>> of their own son, Richard Virenque, probably tells you all you need to know about how good he was.

Of course, every good mountain also needs a bit of drama as well as examples of pure sporting excellence, and the Bonette's sharp-intake-of-breath moment occurred in 2008. John-Lee Augustyn had been first to the top of the Bonette (climbing from the south), but then came a cropper on the way down.

On a sharp right-hand bend he overshot, hit a verge and fell quite some way down the side of the mountain. He was relatively unscathed, but this meant that there was then the pantomime of Augustyn trying to scrabble back up the scree in cycling shoes. The fact that he was being pushed (somewhat indelicately) by a spectator only added to the effect, which was topped off by there being no bike for him to ride when he did regain the road.

The Barloworld rider was forced to stand around waiting for a team car while his Bianchi lay within sight but out of reach below. He did eventually finish the stage, but the infamy of that fall has arguably never left him.

Such is the length of the climb (as you travel in the other direction to Augustyn), and so well hidden is the eventual summit, that you may well begin to wonder if it will ever end. However, as you pass the pretty little Lac des Eissaupres, you can delight or despair in the knowledge that you have about 7km (4⅓ miles) to go.

Half that distance again and you'll be at a fairly large, quite dilapidated flat-roofed stone building. This is an old barracks from the Little Maginot Line, the huge defences built by the French in the 1930s and named after Minister of War André Maginot.

The last section looks almost volcanic, such is the nature of the barren landscape

As you climb higher to the top you'll see other concrete constructions that form part of the Little Maginot Line known as the Ouvrage Restefond.

Generally speaking, hairpins tend to come thick and fast as you approach the highest point of a mountain climb. As the air thins, so a final scramble up to a summit often sees a ladder-like concentration of switchbacks helping you up the final few metres. Which is why it feels odd to have France's highest road within sight and yet be on a relatively straight piece of tarmac. Odder still is that the road tilts back towards flat so that, after 20km (12½ miles) of constant climbing, you suddenly find yourself gaining speed and possibly even shifting up into the big ring.

As you punch through 2,700m (8,858ft) you can conceivably be travelling quite quickly, but sadly this feeling doesn't carry you all the way to the top. If you wish to merely cycle the Col de la Bonette you can stay in the big ring, turn left at 2,715m (8,907ft) and cut through the scree to descend towards Nice.

However, if you want the full 2,802m (9,193ft) Cime de la Bonette experience you'll need to reacquaint yourself with your recently rejected little ring and keep going for a further kilometre that averages close to 10% and spikes to over 15%.

This last section looks almost volcanic, such is the monochromatic nature of the barren landscape. But, if you can, lift your eyes from your immediate surroundings and you'll see the view of the mountains of the Mercantour National Park and beyond. It's the sort of view that is very much befitting of the highest pass in Europe. Even though the Bonette isn't.

Summit height: 1,755m *(5,758ft)*
Altitude gain: 1,168m *(3,832ft)*
Length: 19.1km *(11¾ miles)*
Average gradient: 6%
Maximum gradient: 11.5%

Port de Balès

The scene of one of cycling's most infamous moments, the Port de Balès in the French Pyrenees may look cuddly, but it has a vicious bite.

The banner strung tautly between two buildings declares '*Port de Balès: 19km de bonheur*' with a small abstract picture of some cyclists next to it. Yet, while you might get a warm glow of satisfaction when cresting a summit, the notion that this Pyrenean climb will provide an entire 19km (11¾ miles) of happiness seems a touch unlikely.

You set off from Mauléon-Barousse and, for the first few kilometres, a suspicion creeps over you that just maybe this *will* be unremittingly pleasant, because the gradient is almost nonexistent. The single-lane road, the D925, meanders along the valley floor to the village of Ferrère – a collection of houses that is sleepy on the same level as parents of newborn babies. Look out for the small bus shelter on your right that has some books set into a nook in the wall. You could make your way through quite a few volumes before any transport materializes.

Leaving the comatose metropolis behind, you continue to potter along this leafy lane, with the river Ourse to one side. What appears to be a large, empty, possibly haunted youth hostel appears on your right, then the trees close back in again and there's nothing much more of note to interrupt the sylvan silence until you cross a small bridge with 7km (4⅓ miles) under your wheels.

So far, so 'bonheur', but from this point your level of happiness will be in direct proportion to the strength of your legs, because the final 11.7km (7¼ miles) of the climb averages a stiff 8%. The road feels as though it narrows a little more now, sucking in its sides as it scales the flanks of the valley. A craggy rock face emerges to your right, while the beech trees remain on your left. Although the tarmac twists and turns, it rarely switches back on itself in this section, so the effort feels sustained as you climb.

Such is the wild nature of the road that it's no surprise to learn that it was just a track until the 1980s, and the surface was seemingly only really tidied up in 2006. There is at least some reading material to keep you occupied, although it's mostly a little repetitive, the graffiti artists sticking to their theme with an >>

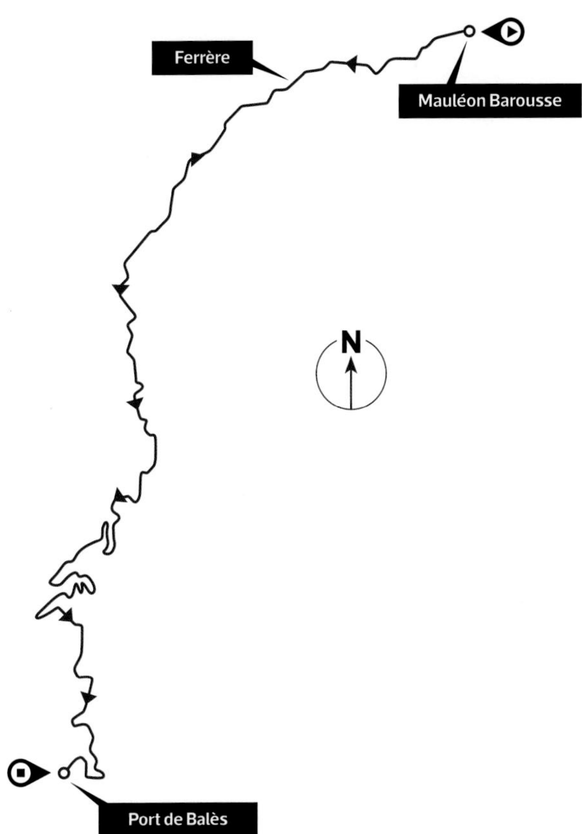

There is at least some reading material…the topic at hand is bears

>> admirable tenacity. The topic at hand is bears, with '*Non a l'ours*' ('No to the bear') being the chosen slogan. It seems local farmers do not want to be sure of a big surprise when they go down to the woods.

Slovenian brown bears were first re-introduced to the Pyrenees in 2006 yet, given their small number, it is unlikely you'll see one. Equally, photos of your cousin's ill-advised 'puce wardrobe' years are also rare and yet the possibility of unearthing one is nonetheless a touch unnerving.

Anyhow, as the altitude piles on, so a few evergreens begin peppering the previously deciduous woodland and when you reach a concentration of hairpins you know you're nearly out of the woods altogether. The final 2km (1¼ miles) is the most spectacular part, and also the scene of the climb's most infamous moment. It occurred in 2010 during its second appearance in the Tour de France (the first having been in 2007), when the race was celebrating 100 years of the Pyrenees' inclusion in the route.

It is Stage 15 and a 25-year-old Andy Schleck of Team Saxo Bank, wearing the yellow jersey, has just attacked out of what remains of the bunch. He's got a gap and only Alexander Vinokourov in the turquoise of Astana seems able to follow. Then, disaster. While pedalling hard, out of the saddle, Schleck's back wheel suddenly hops in the air as his drivetrain jams. He sits, his legs spin uselessly as the speed evaporates and he coasts while looking down at his chain.

It's while Schleck is in this obviously stricken state that Alberto Contador, lying in second place overall, stands on the pedals, almost brushing shoulders with Schleck as he sweeps past. The cameras now show the young Luxembourger off the bike trying once, twice to put his chain back on. Meanwhile, the Spaniard is flying up the road and looks back once, twice towards his immobile rival. By the finish line >>

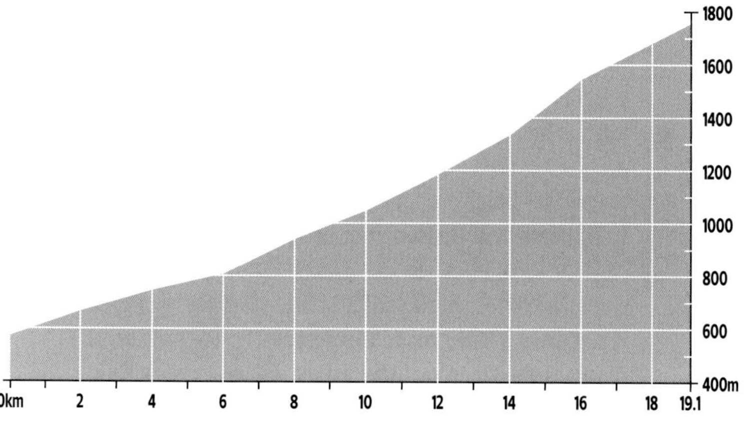

>> in Bagnères-de-Luchon, Contador has taken 39 seconds out of Schleck. The margin between the two in Paris six days later? Perhaps unfortunately, it is exactly 39 seconds.

Opinion remains divided to this day as to whether El Pistolero should have adhered to an unwritten rule and declined to take advantage of the race leader's mechanical issues. Contador certainly tried to absolve himself of any impropriety, claiming after the stage that he was already attacking when the incident occurred (are you attacking or catching up when you're behind?), that he was unaware of Schleck's problem (perhaps he thought Schleck was stopping to examine the wildlife) and that he never looked back (probably just a crick in the neck).

What certainly was against the rules was the level of clenbuterol found in Contador's blood when it was taken two days later. After much explanation

on Contador's part of the cause being dodgy steak, Schleck was eventually declared the winner of the 2010 Tour de France in February 2012.

The controversy stitched the Port de Balès into the tapestry of the Tour, which tends to tackle the climb in this north-south direction. The southern side, which sweeps down past the foot of the Col de Peyresourde, arguably has even better views, but it has never been used in the Tour because the idea of descending this steeper, narrower, rougher and altogether more dangerous northern side in a race is not a particularly pleasant one.

Tackling the final 2km (1¼ miles) to the top is likely to be what you really remember about this climb, because the views over the grassy landscape are stunning and it's dizzying to look back down on the tiny grey scratch of a road on the green slopes below.

At only 1,755m (5,758ft) in height, the Port de Balès isn't a giant and the summit looks more like you've arrived in the Lake District than the French Pyrenees, but it is beautiful. To say that this ride provides 19.1km (11¾ miles) of happiness might be a stretch, but there is something very satisfying and rather special about this quiet climb.

Summit height: 2,000m *(6,562ft)*
Altitude gain: 1,579m *(5,180ft)*
Length: 19.1km *(11¾ miles)*
Average gradient: 8%
Maximum gradient: 11%

Col de la Madeleine

Its name sounds quite inviting, but the Col de la Madeleine in the French Alps is not to be trifled with.

Your first thought is, of course, of food. Was the climb named after a small, shell-like Génoise sponge cake? Certainly, as you make your way up the 19.1km (11¾ miles) from the village of La Chambre, you will need to take on sustenance, and a couple of little madeleines would fit nicely into a jersey pocket, so it would seem appropriate.

But no. The cakes are actually from the Lorraine region of France, a few hundred kilometres to the north. Which is a shame. In fact this climb originally went by a different name, the Col de la Colombe, which in old French means the pass of the dove (and, as a brief aside, helps explain why the Italian brand Columbus tubing has a dove on its badge). The modern name of Col de la Madeleine has two possible origins.

The first, and more likely, is that the col was named after the hospice established by the Cordeliers monks in La Chambre. Not that the hospice was named after Saint Madeleine (patron saint of schoolgirls and only canonized as recently as 1925). Nor was it thought that you might need a hospice after tackling the 8% average gradient. In fact, Madeleine is posited as a corruption of *maladerie*, the old French word for hospice. We'll come to the second option later on, but all this will give you food for thought as you haul yourself up the D213, and you'll need plenty to think about because it is a long climb. Don't be fooled into thinking that its length means this isn't a difficult ascent, because it is.

The gradient, while never ramping up wildly, seems to drag at your legs interminably. The road is also wide, with a white line running confidently down its middle, which lessens the look of the incline and makes you feel as though you ought to be making better progress. Then there is the fact that from near the start you catch glimpses of the sunny uplands that you're heading for at the summit. They look a dispiritingly long way away.

Better, then, to occupy your mind with distracting thoughts, although it would be wise to not trouble yourself with imagining what might be snuffling in the woods that line the road for the majority of the first 14km (8¾ miles). The sight of three boar heads mounted rustically outside a farmhouse might plant >>

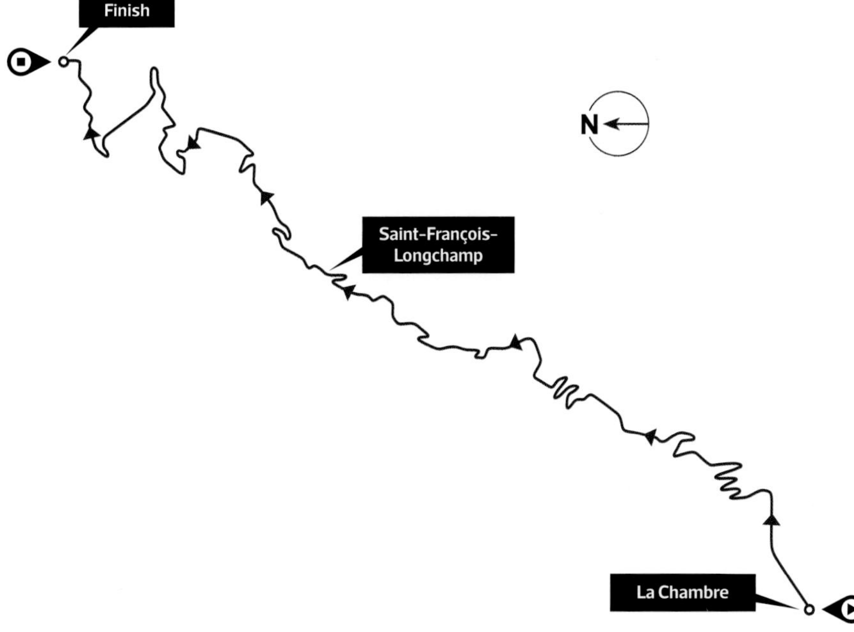

>> the thought of being impaled on some angry tusks. There are also said to be wolves and lynx in the Massif de la Lauzière, within which the Madeleine sits, although the last bear in Savoie was apparently killed here in 1921.

Maybe it's the snuffling or maybe it's because you can often glimpse the rooftops of La Chambre between the trees, or maybe it's the wide, well-surfaced road, but despite there being relatively little traffic, the Madeleine never feels remote and lonely like so many climbs into the mountains. There is a sense that civilization is never too far away.

When you get the chance to look back down towards La Chambre, you get a rather wonderful view across the majestic Maurienne Valley, where – nestled in a partition in the mountains opposite – lies the start of the Col du Glandon.

After around 14km (8¾ miles), the trees thin and then disappear altogether as you reach the small ski town of Saint-François-Longchamp. It's a typical collection of silent ski lifts and ugly flat-roofed buildings with balconies striping every side, but it is also the clear gateway between the lower and upper sections of the climb, because once free of the artless architecture, you find yourself in a completely different setting.

Quite suddenly, you're among *alpages* – the mountain pastures. These havens for wild flowers are carefully maintained, with the herds of cattle, sheep and goats limited in number. If you like dairy products you'll be interested to know that the cows grazing here (Abondance or 'brown and whites', depending on how technical you are with your bovine naming) are some of those responsible for the region's delicious hard cheese, Beaufort.

The landscape in this section is exactly the sort of scenery that you associate with television pictures of the Tour de France, and sure enough the race has regularly been over the *col* since its first appearance in 1969. It is often spoken of in revered tones by professionals, yet it has never had the accolade of hosting a summit finish. It is therefore one of the Tour's ultimate hurdles, standing in the way to sap strength and grind riders down en route to a finish elsewhere, most often on Alpe d'Huez. Two of the sport's great climbers, Lucien Van Impe and Richard Virenque, have led over the summit of the pass three times, and their pedigree rather cements the Madeleine as a real test of ascension.

The summit is certainly something to be savoured. The final 200m (219yd) to the crest of the road is arrow straight and as you crawl or sprint up it, depending on your energy levels and motivation, the sight that greets you on a clear day is truly magnificent. Seemingly rising out of the tarmac with each centimetre in altitude gained is the snow-capped peak of Mont Blanc. It's quite possible that you will never get a better view of it, nor see quite so clearly how its 4,808-m (15,774-ft) summit towers over everything around it.

Talking of heights, the Madeleine used to be listed as 1,993m (6,539ft) in height. But then the 2012 Tour rolled around and it was reset to 2,000m (6,562ft) exactly, a figure perpetuated by the name of La Banquise 2000, the lone restaurant standing at the top.

All of which brings us neatly to that second possible origin of the assignation Madeleine, because the eatery at the top of the *col* is built on the site of a chapel dedicated to Mary Magdalene, and Madeleine is the modern version of Magdalene. If you're lucky, you'll be able to pick up some of the cakes, too.

Summit height: 1,912m *(6,273ft)*
Altitude gain: 1,582m *(5,190ft)*
Length: 21.4km *(13¼ miles)*
Average gradient: 7.5%
Maximum gradient: 12%

Mont Ventoux

As famous for its barren moonscape as for the tales of death and glory that have played out on its slopes, Ventoux has a claim to be the most legendary climb in cycling.

It's like a three-course meal. You start with something light and easy on the stomach, then you move to the main course, a big portion of stew with one too many dumplings. And the final course is also rich, but simultaneously refreshing and a feast for the eyes. Perhaps a raspberry pavlova.

Likewise, climbing Mont Ventoux in the south of France can definitely be split into three very distinct portions. In fact, you could probably add a fourth – perhaps a pre-meal *amuse bouche* – because so great is this mountain's reputation that the anticipation of climbing the Giant of Provence dominates your thinking long before you hit the road.

You can see its apparently snowy peak rising intimidatingly from the landscape all the way from the A7 Autoroute to the west. You then have another 45 minutes of driving to contemplate it before you >>

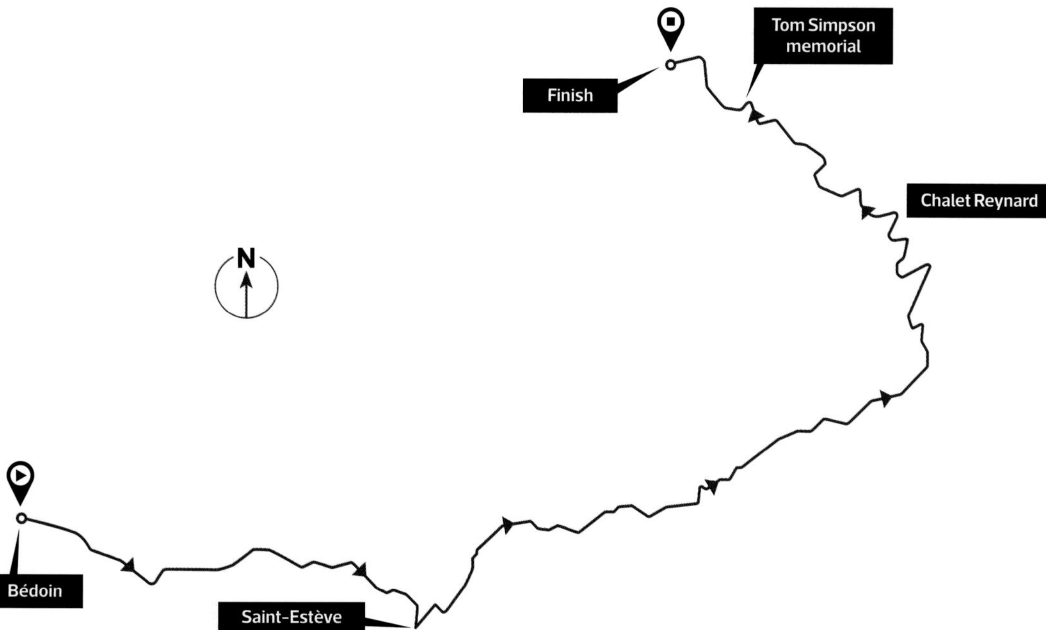

>> even reach the foot of the climb. Actually, Ventoux's peak isn't covered in snow for most of the year. It merely appears that way because of the bare, bleached limestone that covers the top (pudding) section. But all that is to come.

The start of the climb is down among the honey-coloured walls of Bédoin, a bustling little town commercially as well as physically dominated by the mountain in whose shadow it sits. If you turn up without a spare tube or lacking a sugary sachet, there are plenty of places happy to sell you such things, along with a commemorative jersey.

There are in fact three towns from which you can begin an ascent of Ventoux, the other locations being Malaucène to the north and Sault to the east. But it's the climb from Bédoin that is the toughest in terms of gradient and most notorious thanks to its appearances in the Tour de France. Not that the gradient is particularly arduous to start with, as you pedal easily between the vineyards. The incline averages just 4% for the first 5km (3 miles).

The second portion of the climb starts on a big left-hand hairpin at Saint-Estève, with a rather delicious-looking restaurant on the outside of the corner. If you somehow miss the fact that you've gone round a large left-hand hairpin, you'll know you are in the second act by the advent of mixed woodland, which brings strong smells of sap and a stultifying denseness to the air on a hot day.

The next 9.6km (6 miles) – your main course – average a gruelling 9% and there really is no rest. The road meanders in such a way as to tease you into thinking that perhaps something easier lies just out of sight, but it doesn't. Curiously, the small stone >>

2000 1800 1600 1400 1200 1000 800 600 400 200m

0km 2 4 6 8 10 12 14 16 18 20 21.4

From the eerie stillness to the spectral wind, this mountain feels unsettling

>> distance markers are all on the left-hand side of the road, which means they're easily missed. A bike computer is invaluable on this ride, because otherwise it's very hard to know how far there is to go.

It was near the end of this middle section that the Chris Froome farce took place in 2016. The stage had been shortened due to strong winds on the highest part of the mountain, and Thomas De Gendt had already soloed to victory, when a combination of crowds and motorbikes formed an unintentional blockade into which the hapless Richie Porte crashed. Unable to take evasive action, Froome piled into the Australian and snapped his Pinarello into the bargain. Stricken and panicked, Froome bailed on the broken bike and began clattering up the road on his cleats.

The finish line that day was at Chalet Reynard, where the ascent from Sault on the D164 joins the D974. A cafe selling yet more commemorative clothing (as well as food) is a tempting place to stop, but if you can resist, the road sweeps left across a car park that feels bewilderingly large after the confines of the trees, and on to the third and final section of the climb.

Averaging 8% for 6.1km (3¾ miles), this last leg might not appear vastly different from the previous one. However, the cooler air, the distracting views, the alien landscape, the hairpins and the red-and-white carrot of a visible finishing point at the top all combine to make it feel somehow less arduous.

That's not to say this curious final sector, with its limestone landscape poking above the trees like a vast compound fracture in the earth, doesn't have its difficulties. For a start, the infamous Mistral wind can make it hard to stay upright on some days and the exposure is evident even if the wind is calm, seemingly either baking you under a grill-like sun or chilling you to the bone.

It was that intense heat that got to 29-year-old Tom Simpson in 1967. The amphetamines and alcohol in his system probably didn't help, but it seems unlikely that they alone would have toppled Britain's original cycling hero. Deliriously determined to reach the finish, Simpson died on the slopes of Ventoux during Stage 13 of the Tour de France. Today, the grey granite memorial to him that stands at the side of the road near where he collapsed shows just how agonizingly close to the top he was. It seems as though you can almost reach out and touch the buildings above you, although in reality there is still one last sucker punch of a double-digit gradient to be overcome.

The thought of Simpson throws a slightly sombre shroud over the final push for the summit, although there is a curious atmosphere the whole way up the climb. From the eerie stillness among the trees, where it's easy to feel you're being watched, to the spectral wind that tugs at wheels and whips mist across the wild upper slopes, it's a mountain that seems slightly unsettling.

It's not a feeling alleviated by the buildings at the top, which have the air of an empty prison about them. But although the late 19th-century meteorological station and 1960s telecommunications mast are ugly, it's thanks to that weather station that the road was built in the first place. And it's obvious why they were built here: on a clear day the view is as expansive as from the top of any traditional Alpine or Pyrenean climb. A feast for the eyes, no less.

Summit height: 2,642m *(8,668ft)*
Altitude gain: 1,208m *(3,963ft)*
Length: 17.7km *(11 miles)*
Average gradient: 6.9%
Maximum gradient: 12.1%

Col du Galibier

Since its Tour de France debut in 1911, the Galibier has dared riders to test themselves on its fearsome slopes.

To describe the Galibier as the oldest Alpine climb is misleading. After all, the paths over the Alps existed long before the Tour de France arrived, and who knows which appeared first? However, in terms of the Tour, the Galibier is the most senior of all the Alpine climbs and it has a grandeur befitting this status.

It debuted in 1911, just a year after the Tourmalet had first ushered high mountains into the race. A famous photo of that day shows Gustav Garrigou pushing his bike up a muddy, deeply rutted track between banks of snow. It is the sort of photo that saps the energy just by looking at it. And in case you think that the trudging Garrigou was some sort of also-ran, he won the Tour that year.

Today, despite a considerably better surface and little likelihood of snow in summer, the Galibier remains a formidable challenge to pros and amateurs alike. Whichever side you tackle it from, you will already have some climbing in your legs by the time you begin the ascent, because it can only be accessed on its northern side via the Col du Telegraphe (11.8km/ 7 1/3 miles at 7.3%) or on its southern side by the Col de Lauteret (34.2km/21 1/4 miles at 3.8%).

The more popular and testing side – and the side used in 1911 – is from the north, and it begins in the ski resort of Valloire. Starting a climb somewhere high enough to host winter sports, knowing that >>

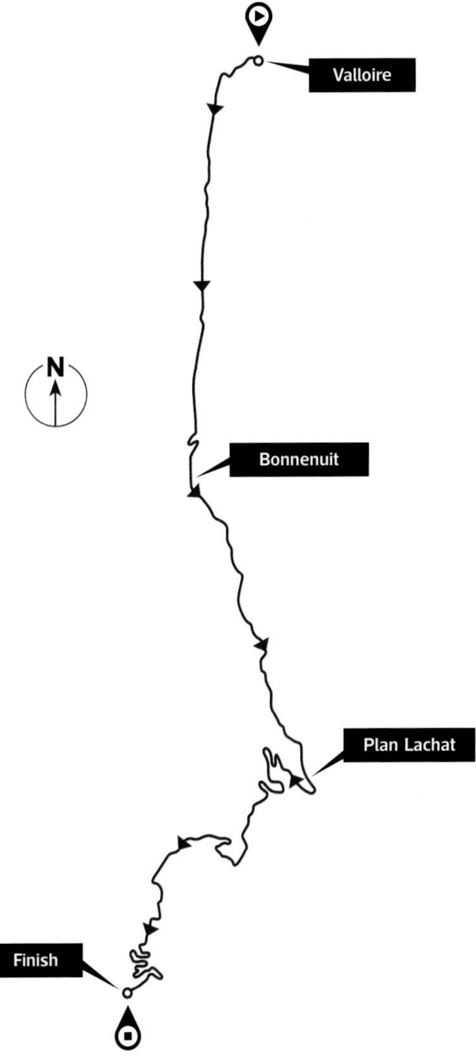

>> you have 18km (11 miles) and 1,200m (3,937ft) of vertical ascent ahead of you, means you are definitely heading into rarefied air. As if to reinforce this point, the small chapel you pass on the outskirts of Valloire is dedicated to St Bernard, patron saint of mountaineers.

An aerial view of the road shows a route that looks as though someone is halfway through unravelling the Christmas lights. The first 10km (6¼ miles) to Plan Lachet via Bonnenuit is almost straight as it climbs up the valley of the river Valloirette. At ground level you'll find there is actually a gentle meander to this section of the climb (plus two hairpins just before Bonnenuit), so you never see the vast distances up the road ahead that the view from above would suggest. In terms of gradient, this first section averages 6%, but that includes about 2.5km (1½ miles) of rather false flat.

As you near the second half of the climb (the tangled bit that makes you swear you'll put the lights away more carefully this year), the buildings dwindle and vast grey scree slopes on the other side of the valley give a menacing air to the landscape. Then, at Plan Lachat, there is a right-hand hairpin across a bridge spanning the river where the road instantly kicks up to 9% and stays there for more than 3km (1¾ miles). Not that things have been easy so far, but it suddenly feels as though the warm-up is over as three switchbacks lift you out of the valley and into a green landscape sprinkled with grey rocks.

This is where Julian Alaphilippe – going in the opposite direction – valiantly clung on to the yellow jersey in the 2019 Tour de France. Having been dropped on the southern ascent, he made up a 20-second deficit with a breathtaking display of descending, catching his rivals and then scything through their ranks.

There has been some wonderful flair shown in the face of gravity, too. In 1952, Fausto Coppi cemented his position at the front of the race (which he would go on to win by more than 28 minutes) by attacking with 15km (9⅓ miles) to go on the Galibier. By the summit, his lead was nearly three minutes, and by the stage finish in Sestriere he was seven minutes clear. Tour director Jacques Goddet said, 'Coppi climbing is like a ski-lift gliding up its steel cable.'

Then there was Marco Pantani in 1998, attacking in the rain, hands on the drops, wearing a blue bandana and riding a bike with yellow tyres. He flew out of the peloton 11km (6¾ miles) from the summit of the Galibier and 48km (30 miles) from the finish in Les Deux Alpes. He seemed to hesitate after his initial burst, almost stopping to look back over his shoulder, but seeing no reaction from behind he set off into >>

>> the clouds. He finished nine minutes ahead of yellow jersey wearer and defending champion Jan Ullrich to take a race lead he would hold until Paris.

With about 4km ($2\frac{1}{2}$ miles) to go, you pass a couple of buildings and enter a huge, lumpy, grassy bowl, and if the weather is better than it was on that day in 1998 you can see to your left the 3,228-m (10,590-ft) peak of the Grand Galibier that gives the col its name.

The end of the climb will also now be in sight, and it's quite an end. Until 1976, the summit was at 2,556m (8,386ft) and the peloton went through a 365-m (1,197-ft) tunnel below the crest, emerging where a monument to Desgrange now stands. However, when the tunnel was closed for refurbishment in 1976, a new section of road was laid over the top of the ridge, taking the summit of the col to 2,642m (8,668ft). When the tunnel was finally reopened in 2002, cyclists were no longer allowed through it, the exception being Stage 19 of the 2011 Tour, which celebrated 100 years of the Galibier's first inclusion in the race by crossing it on consecutive days in each direction.

The final stretch to the new summit is really tough. The road is narrower than the rest of the climb and the Galibier hits its steepest incline of 12.1%. Combined with the altitude, it's enough to drain any remaining vestiges of power from your legs. Sprint for the line out of the last hairpin and you're likely to find yourself back in the saddle before you get there.

Once at the top, though, you stand on a summit that is historically and geographically the epicentre of the Alps as far as the Tour is concerned, because at every point of the compass around you there lies another famous road that has helped shape the race's history. Climbs really don't come much more classic than the Galibier.

2600
2400
2200
2000
1800
1600
1400m
0km 2 4 6 8 10 12 14 16 17.7

Croix de Fer

In the pantheon of Alpine climbs, the Col de la Croix de Fer is often wrongly overlooked.

There would be every temptation to think of the Col de la Croix de Fer as second tier in the ranks of Classic Climbs. The route from the southwest suggests an underwhelming average gradient of just over 5% for the 24.3km (15 miles). The summit crests 2,000m but only just, at 2,067m (6,781ft).

What's more, the ascent is only used in the Tour de France as a softener before nearby Alpe d'Huez or La Toussuire. It's not even the grandest route to the bottom of the Alpe, as it is often side-stepped in favour of the more glamorous Col du Galibier. Yet to overlook the Croix de Fer – the Pass of the Iron Cross – is akin to walking straight past Caravaggio's *Death of the Virgin* simply to get to the *Mona Lisa* when you visit the Louvre. You are missing out on a masterpiece in its own right.

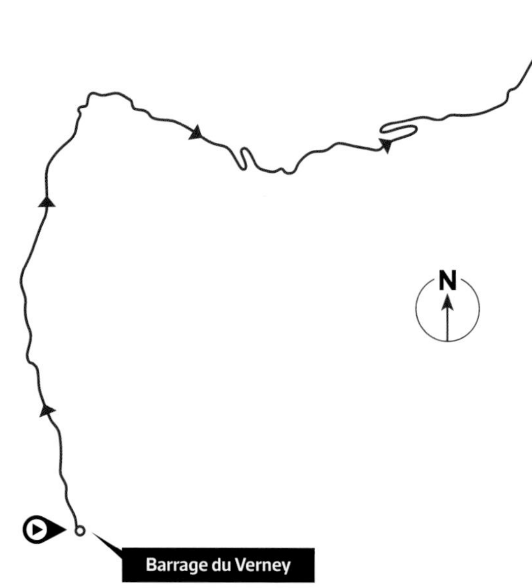

The climb begins next to the first of the ascent's two huge dams, the Barrage du Verney. A couple of hairpins lead up the face of the dam and then the road runs along the very top of it before turning left and bridging the beautiful body of water that lies behind it. At the northern end, you are greeted by an imposing, brutalist, Bond-villain-style building, and the air hums and crackles menacingly as you pass, thanks to the wires attached to concrete masts outside. Welcome to France's largest hydroelectric power station.

The D526 circles behind the building, descends briefly, then heads roughly due north for the next 7km (4¹/₃ miles). This section of the climb is reminiscent of the middle portion of Mont Ventoux from Saint-Estève to Chalet Reynard in that you climb through trees and the road meanders, without any true switchbacks to break things up. It gets harder too, the gradient creeping up insidiously from around 6% initially to over 9%. It's like wading out to sea from the beach: initially the waves present little resistance, but the deeper you go, the harder each stride gets.

It was here among the trees that Alberto Contador bounced away from the main peloton in familiar style during Stage 17 of the 2017 Tour de France. This was El Pistolero's final season as a pro and he seemed to spend the Tour trying to go out in an attacking blaze of glory. It was a tactic that didn't garner many results (in the end he was well beaten by Primož Roglič on Stage 17), but it did spice up the action. >>

>> **Suddenly there's a blissful easing of the incline** and a whole kilometre of flat road rewards you for your efforts. What could be better? Well, how about a descent? As the road dips down, you can see across to where the climb continues up through steep-sided valleys, but first – for 1.5km (1 mile) and four delightful hairpins – you drop down to a small bridge over the Eau d'Olle, a tributary of the Rhône via the Romanche.

As you cross the small bridge, revelling in the cool breeze afforded by the speed of your gravity-assisted plummet, you'd do well to change down gears. Possibly all the way down, because in the blink of an eye you go from merrily freewheeling to standing up on the pedals and heaving on the handlebars as you lean into a gradient in the mid-teens. The contrast between descent and ascent means you smash into the steepest part of the Croix de Fer like you've hit a wall. If you haven't changed down in anticipation, neither your chain nor your legs will thank you.

The gradient stays in double digits for the next 2km (1¼ miles), the road threading along a vertiginous and winding valley. After a while, the road throws in a couple of hairpins for the sake of variety and after

In the blink of an eye you go from freewheeling to standing up on the pedals

another couple of kilometres it opens out to reveal the second dam of the day. Constructed between 1978 and 1985 (perhaps explaining the Croix de Fer's reappearance in the 1986 Tour de France after a 20-year absence), this is the Grand'Maison Dam, an embankment dam standing 140m (459ft) high and designed to hold back the 140 million cubic metres of water that the Lac de Grand'Maison can store.

Another pair of hairpins brings you up level with the top of the structure and then you're treated to the most wonderful run along the left bank of the lake. The gradient is pleasant to non-existent and the view is magnificent. It's as if a miniature fjord has been trapped high in the Alps, such is the way that the steep slopes angle into the water. >>

>> **The climb's second descent lasts the same 1.5km** (1 mile) as the first but is different in character, swapping switchbacks for a succession of shallow bends that can be taken at speed. Incidentally, the start of the descent marks the otherwise imperceptible point where you cross from the Isère to the Savoie department and the road changes from the D526 to the D926.

From here to the top is just over 5km (3 miles) and the gradient averages 6.5%, which allows you to admire your sumptuous surroundings. The road to the summit of the Col du Glandon (D927) will appear on your left, but push on instead along the road that you can see clinging to the left-hand side of the majestic grassy valley ahead. It is a beautiful final few kilometres, the mountains feeling friendly rather than frightening, yet still imposing and impressive.

And then you see it, smaller and more delicate than you might imagine, perched atop a roughly carved, or perhaps just weathered, stone column. Somehow fragile in among all the vast jagged peaks: the iron cross. The summit is neither deserted nor bustling with commerce, but there is a remoteness to it, as there should be with a mountain pass.

Then there are the views. With the jagged Aiguilles d'Arves standing proud on the horizon ahead and the softer vista of the vast valley behind you, there is variety as well as pure grandeur. In fact, the variety is perhaps the most pleasing thing about the whole climb. The captivating contrast – of ups and downs, hard and easy, the confined and the expansive – means there is nothing second tier about the experience of climbing the Croix de Fer.

2000
1500
1000
500
0m
0km
5
10
15
20
24.3

Summit height: 1,709m *(5,607ft)*
Altitude gain: 1,190m *(3,904ft)*
Length: 16.6km *(10⅓ miles)*
Average gradient: 7.2%
Maximum gradient: 13%

Col d'Aubisque

So often the bridesmaid to the Tourmalet, the Col d'Aubisque can still stand among the greats of the world's cycling climbs.

On a sunny day, with vast green slopes close at hand and picturesque mountainscapes beyond, the Col d'Aubisque is one of the most peaceful and beautiful places in the world. As you climb its steep but stunning final slopes, the only blip in the total calm is likely to be the sound of your breathing. It's the same with many other climbs, of course, but here it is hard to comprehend that this oasis in the Pyrenees has been the scene of some of the most thrilling action in bike racing.

Its serenity is amplified by the fact that it doesn't feature high up most lists of 'must-do climbs', thanks to its bridesmaid status to the nearby Tourmalet. For example, the Aubisque was there on 21 July 1910 when the high mountains were first included in the Tour de France, but it was the second mountain to be climbed after the Tourmalet. It was at the top of the Aubisque that Octave Lapize, winner of the Tour in 1910, famously shouted at the organizers, '*Vous êtes des assassins*! yet it is at the top of the Tourmalet that his statue rests today.

When the spotlight has swung onto the Aubisque, it's often been a stage that has provided incredible drama. Take Stage 16 of the 2007 Tour, which finished on this summit for only the third time. The day began with Kazakh rider Alexander Vinokourov leaving the race after it was discovered his blood had been tampered with. (He denied any wrongdoing but was banned from competing for two years by the UCI.) Then, an incredible battle between Michael Rasmussen in the yellow jersey, a young Alberto Contador in the white, Levi Leipheimer and Cadel Evans.

Contador kept springing away with thrilling, stinging attacks, but Rabobank's Rasmussen brought him back every time. Leipheimer, Contador's Discovery teammate, was on the offensive too and Evans was a lurking, grinding menace. But nobody could break the Dane and with a kilometre to go he distanced them all, crossing the line first and tightening his grasp on yellow.

Yet there were boos from the crowd as Rasmussen mounted the podium on top of this spectacular mountain pass. The reason for the heckling was that he had missed doping tests before the Tour; in addition, the previous night, fresh allegations came to light that he hadn't missed the pre-Tour tests because he was in Mexico as he had claimed. Despite his denial of any wrongdoing, the Dane was expelled from the Tour by his team.

If that day in 2007 provided as much controversy as captivating action on the road, 3 September 2016 was all about the racing. This was not the Tour de France, but the Vuelta a España that finished atop the Aubisque. First, there was the feel-good story of >>

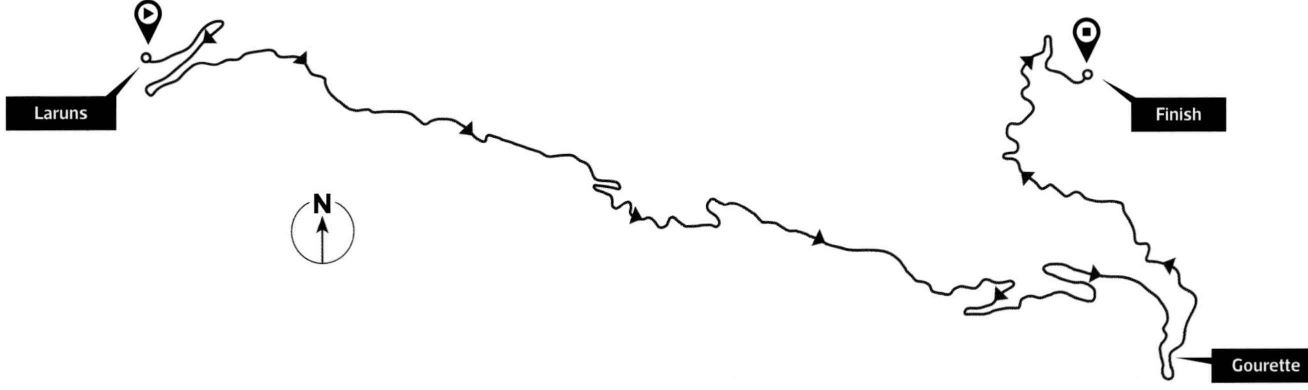

>> the winner on the day. Dutchman Robert Gesink, afflicted by numerous injuries during his career and even the recipient of heart surgery in 2014, finally crossed the line in front of everyone else on a Grand Tour stage. Then, there was the action behind him. While Nairo Quintana and Chris Froome were battling for the overall lead, Orica-BikeExchange decided to go on the rampage. Having placed three riders in the break, Simon Yates then attacked over the top of the Col de Marie-Blanque, meeting up with his teammates in the valley so they could lead him out to the Aubisque. It was beautifully executed and the move produced a thrilling day's racing.

On both of those occasions, the peloton ascended from the west. Although the climbing starts in Laruns, things really get going about 3km (1¾ miles) outside the centre of the village as you swing off the D934 onto the D918. It's a wide road, but you are mainly cloistered by the trees at this point.

The small settlement of Eaux-Bonnes (good waters) would seem like an excellent place to top up on refreshment, although you're subjected to a curious tour round a one-way system that goes up and round a park as you follow the road. After this brief glimpse of civilization, it's back into the trees and a gradient of just over 6%. Another 3km (1¾ miles) further on, however, you reach the steepest pitch of the climb (around 13%) and from here to the top the average incline is a punishing 8%. The only bit where the >>

>> slope seems to relent is as you round a big left-hand hairpin at the ski resort of Gourette with about 4km (2½ miles) to go. After this, you head back into the trees for a kilometre, but then you're released into the beautiful uplands for the final push to the summit.

It's not a climb that's abundant with hairpins, but the ones it has seem to stand out, notably the one on which the Restaurant Les Crêtes Blanches (the white crests) perches. After you've rounded this switchback, the drop to the left recedes a little. You still feel as though you're high up in the mountains, thanks to the peaks on the other side of the Ossau Valley, but the road moves away from any precipitous edges.

At the top, you won't be short of room to stretch out because there's a vast car park that flows off into the distance like a tarmac infinity pool, while the summit is also notable for the huge yellow, polka-dot and green bicycles that stand next to the road. A couple of cafes are also on hand for refreshment and it would seem wise to fortify yourself before the descent, so as not to re-enact the Aubisque's most famous incident...

In 1951, Wim van Est, the first Dutchman to wear the yellow jersey, plummeted towards Tarbes trying to catch those ahead. He crashed twice and on the second occasion fell so far into a ravine that he looked as small as 'a buttercup in the grass', said teammate Gerard Peters. His team had to sacrifice 40 tyres knotted together to a towrope to haul him out, dazed but relatively unscathed.

It's better to emulate flying Dutchman Robert Gesink rather than flying Dutchman Wim Van Est if you tackle the Aubisque.

1800
1500
1200
900
600
300
0m
0km 2 4 6 8 10 12 14 16 16.6

Col de l'Iseran

The highest col in the Alps has had surprisingly few visits from the Tour de France, but it proved to be pivotal when the peloton attacked its slopes in 2019.

There's a philosophical quandary attributed to 18th-century thinker George Berkeley that asks, 'If a tree falls in a forest and no one is around to hear it, does it make a sound?' Similarly, if a rider crosses a finish line that they don't realize they're crossing, is it actually a finish line? And if there is no stage winner, then did the stage even take place?

These and many other questions arose in the 2019 Tour de France, when the Col de l'Iseran became the summit finish that nobody knew was a summit finish. This col is the highest pass in the Alps (despite some protestations from those who live near the Col de la Bonette), soaring to 2,764m (9,068ft) above sea level, or 2,770m (9,088ft) if you believe the sign at the top. Either way, it just beats the Stelvio's 2,757m (9,045ft), and yet curiously the Iseran is nothing like as famous or revered as its Italian rival.

The Iseran's first appearance in the Tour was in 1938, just a year after the road was completed, but in the subsequent 82 years it appeared in the race a scant seven more times. Still, the *col*'s most (in)famous contribution to Tour history was an unforgettable one. As the peloton set out for Stage 19 in 2019, the Iseran was the penultimate climb on the schedule before the final ramp up to Tignes. Julian Alaphilippe had France in the palm of his hand and the yellow jersey on his back. Every time the race headed into the mountains, people thought he would crack, yet somehow he had held on to his lead, which remained at a reasonable 1 minute 30 seconds.

Now, with just two real stages remaining, Team Ineos were worried the Frenchman might perform a miracle and break the team's remarkable run of success, so they set about making the race as hard as possible on the slopes of the Iseran. After a train of red and black jerseys had performed the usual lead-out duties, Geraint Thomas attacked first with 6km (3¾ miles) to go to the summit. His blow wasn't enough to unship Alaphilippe, but when Jumbo-Visma's Steven Kruijswijk went over the top of Thomas, the Frenchman finally came unstuck. Then, Ineos's Egan Bernal attacked and nobody could hold the young Colombian's wheel. >>

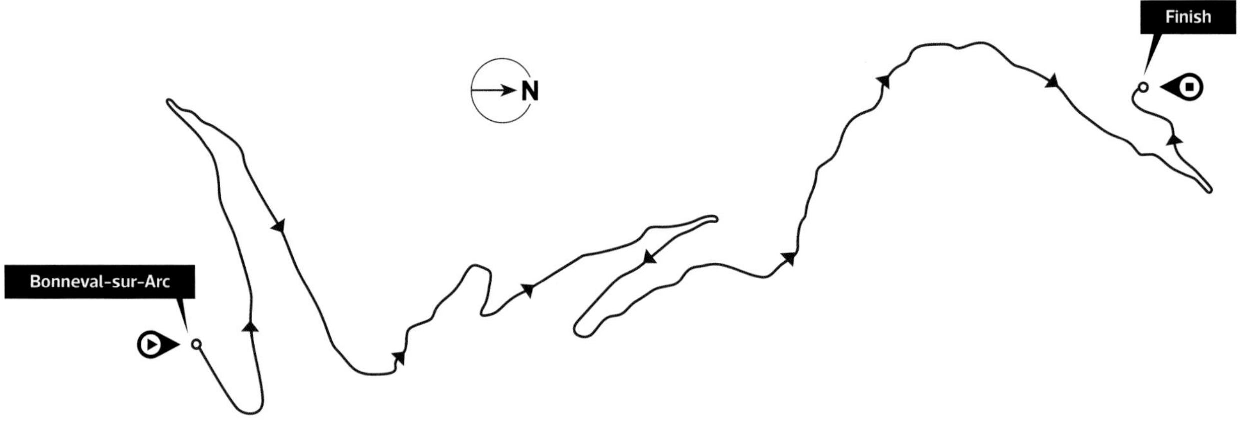

Summit height: 2,764m *(9,068ft)*
Altitude gain: 977m *(3,205ft)*
Length: 13.4km *(8 1/3 miles)*
Average gradient: 7.3%
Maximum gradient: 13%

D 902
COL DE L'ISERAN
ALTITUDE : 2770M
VAL D'ISERE 17
Bg St MAURICE 50

>> The attacks were made all the more spectacular by the scenery. Some climbs tend to pack all the best vistas into the final few kilometres, but on its southern side the Iseran has full high-definition visuals from the start in Bonneval-sur-Arc.

You could say that the climb actually begins way back in Lanslebourg-Mont-Cenis, 33km (20½ miles) from the summit, but seeing as 12km (7½ miles) of that averages less than 1% as you pedal through the vast and beautiful Arc valley, it seems better to concentrate on the final 13.4km (8⅓ miles), which averages 7.3% despite a couple of interludes in the incline.

Bonneval-sur-Arc is a picturesque collection of chalets that's Swiss-like in its charm, and it has indeed been used as a film set. It is officially recognized by an association called Les Plus Beaux Villages de France – the only village in the Savoie department to achieve such an honour. The climb itself kicks off on a big left-hand hairpin and instantly rises up to over 8%, where it stays for the next 4km (2½ miles). As the road rises up above the rooftops, you almost instantly feel the remoteness set in.

The road has no barriers and few markings, giving it a wonderfully wild feel. You'll almost certainly spot marmots on the slopes, but there is also the sort of stillness that you only get when you are a decent distance from civilization.

When the road swings round north into the Vallon de la Lenta, you actually descend for a short distance, but all too soon the road kicks up again into another set of long zigzags. Geraint Thomas's kick came out of this section's second hairpin, which has a lonely, dishevelled building on the outside and signals the start of a kilometre that averages 10.5% and takes you through 2,300m (7,546ft) in altitude. Even as the biggest bike race in the world tackled the slopes that >>

The road has no barriers and few markings, giving it a wonderfully wild feel

>> day the spectators were startlingly sparse, lending a bygone look to the images beamed around the world.

The second, easier section allows you to really pick up speed, despite a big drop to the left. Near the end is a short, slightly random tunnel before you cross a bridge into the bottom of the final valley that leads you up to the edge of the Espace Killy ski area, which covers Tignes and Val d'Isère. From here to the summit you're more than 2,500m (8,202ft) above sea level and the gradient averages 9%. The road also widens a little, which lessens the look of the incline but does nothing to soften its blow.

The final hairpin is majestic and gives you a few revolutions of recovery before the last 800m (2,625ft) to the summit. All the way up, the road has sporadic small red flags with a white cross, and on this last left-hander there's one more tattooed on the tarmac. This is the Savoie's flag.

Then, as you ascend the final ramp, the graffiti suddenly kicks in with a vengeance, with big road-spanning flags, jerseys and exhortations all the way to the finish line...that wasn't a finish line on 26 July 2019. At least not one that Egan Bernal was aware of.

As the race went over the top of the climb on that stage, it also went past the highest chapel in France: Notre Dame de Toute Prudence. And the race organizer ASO did indeed show prudence on Stage 19, calling a halt to proceedings while Bernal, Thomas, Simon Yates, et al. were descending the D902 towards the famous ski resorts. Unbeknown to the riders, a huge storm had covered the road up ahead in hailstones and caused a landslide that made the route impassable.

The result was that the times (even though there was no timing gear) were taken from the top of the previous climb, catapulting Bernal into the yellow jersey, which he would wear all the way to Paris. And thus, the Iseran unwittingly hosted a summit finish. Better late than never.

2800
2400
2000
1600m
0km 2 4 6 8 10 12 13.4

The Rest of the World

St Gotthard Pass

Hairpins, cobbles, Alpine scenery – it's almost as if Switzerland's St Gotthard Pass were made just for cyclists.

It's rare to have such a good view of a road without a hang glider. But it's almost as though the newer, larger road over the St Gotthard Pass was built in the 1970s purely to offer the best vista of the older road built in 1830. Looking southeast from a convenient layby near the top of the new road, you are presented with a panorama over a set of switchbacks so spectacularly serpentine that it looks like an art installation.

What you can see are 24 hairpins crammed into just 4km (2½ miles) of road. It's a view that encapsulates what most people imagine an Alpine pass to look like: a fairytale depiction as much as an engineering feat. You are actually looking across the Val Tremola (trembling valley) at the Tremolastrasse (trembling road), which are appropriate names, because what you can't see from a distance is that the old road is cobbled, so when you ride up it you really do tremble.

The ride begins all the way back down in the village of Airolo. This relatively small municipality in the Italian-speaking Swiss canton of Ticino has seen its fair share of action over the years, precisely because of its location at the foot of the busy pass, its population reaching a zenith in the late 19th century when the first Gotthard rail tunnel was being built. This was an endeavour that saw the first large-scale use of dynamite, but sadly also saw the death of many of those who strove to build it, including its lead engineer, who had a heart attack inside the tunnel.

Today, the mountains are riddled with tunnels like a Swiss cheese, because there are no fewer than three routes going through rather than over. The rail tunnel was the first to be built and at the time was the longest tunnel in the world at 15km (9⅓ miles) in length. In 1980, the road tunnel was completed and that became the longest road tunnel in the world. Then, in 2016, came the Base Tunnel, the world's longest rail and deepest traffic tunnel. There is a lot going on beneath you as you pedal from Via S Gottardo in Airolo to begin the climb.

The first 6km (3¾ miles) are spent ascending the northern side of the Valle Leventina and the old road is interlaced with the new one, the two ribbons of tarmac weaving over and under each other like the >>

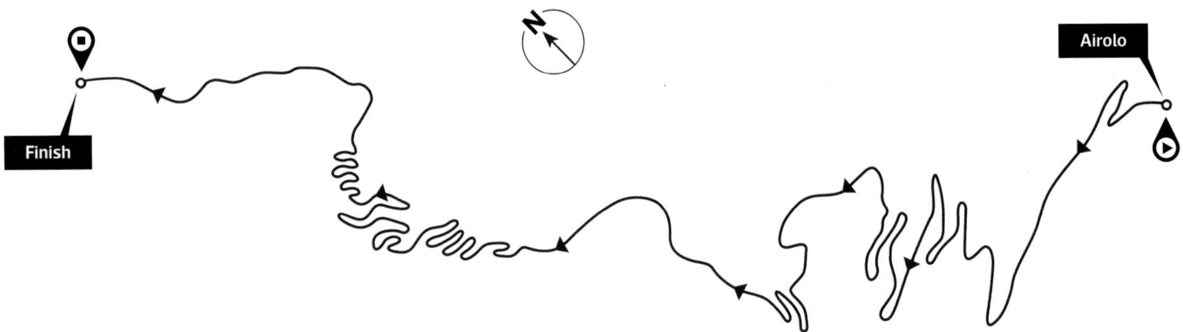

Summit height: 2,108m *(6,916ft)*
Altitude gain: 949m *(3,113½ft)*
Length: 13.8km *(8½ miles)*
Average gradient: 7.5%
Maximum gradient: 11.5%

>> last two strands of spaghetti in the bowl. There are a couple of short cobbled stretches, just to prepare you for what's to come, but the road is mostly smooth and relatively wide. You can tell you're entering the second half of the climb because the cobbles return in earnest, the river Foss begins to hug the road on your right and the land rises up on both sides. There is also a curious concrete structure that looks like a large modernist pavilion, which is actually a vent for one of the tunnels.

The old road is interlaced with the new one like two strands of spaghetti

A word about the cobbles. These aren't the rough rocks of the Trouée d'Arenberg at Paris-Roubaix. They're not even the tighter-knit *pavé* of the Paterberg on the Tour of Flanders. The Tremola's timbre is more regular, with smaller stones arranged incredibly neatly in a fanned pattern, with a thin red line of bricks marking the middle. The road is like a mosaic. You still have to keep half an eye out for imperfections that might derail you, but the sensation of cycling across them is definitely more tremble than serious shudder and you shouldn't have to worry unduly about fitting wider rubber or dropping tyre pressures. Even so, when the pros come here for the Tour de Suisse, you'll see them seeking out the smooth strips at the side of the road. Just watch Egan Bernal's winning attack during Stage 7 of the 2019 race for a good example.

There is about a kilometre of meandering road before you reach the flurry of famous hairpins. On the approach, you cross the Foss so that it is now on >>

Huge curved stone walls tower over you, stacked like tiers on a cake

>> your left. Then, the bends arrive and they are almost as impressive seen from beneath as they are viewed from above. Huge, curved stone walls tower over you, stacked up like tiers on a cake, each one supporting a switchback. It's quite intimidating and there is a feeling of mounting the ramparts to some mountain fortress.

The average gradient for the climb is 7.5%, but it fluctuates a fair bit and the relatively wide, flat hairpins offer an opportunity to rest. Nonetheless, the steepest part of the whole climb arrives not long after you have begun the *tornanti* (hairpins) and sees the road pitch up to average over 11% for around 200m (219yd), which is more than enough to have you searching for a bit of extra help from your gears.

One thing you don't have to contend with is a lot of traffic. Some is underground, but the rest is diverted across to the other side of the valley in the avalanche tunnel that bisects the grey and green scenery like a zip. It means the Gotthard is a peaceful as well as a picturesque climb. At least until you reach the top.

The dizzying hairpins actually end about a kilometre from the summit. As you head up the final straight ramp with the cheery Lago dei Morti (Lake of the Dead) on your right, you see the gaggle of buildings at the top, which remind you what an important way through the mountains this has been since Roman times. St Gotthard's past certainly justifies the presence of the medium-sized museum at the top. Even if you have no appetite for a history lesson, you'll probably be hungry for whatever the restaurant is serving.

Or maybe you'll simply pass the impressive, eagle-festooned monument to pilot Adrien Guex, who crashed his Fokker here in 1927, and head on down into the German-speaking canton of Uri. The lure of the descent on the northern side is that it is one of the fastest anywhere in the Alps. You might want to stick to the modern, non-cobbled road this time, though. There are fewer trembles that way.

Vršič Pass

Summit height: 1,611m *(5,285ft)*

Altitude gain: 761m *(2,497ft)*

Length: 9.3km *(5¾ miles)*

Average gradient: 8.2%

Maximum gradient: 12.5%

Mangart

Summit height: 2,055m *(6,742ft)*

Altitude gain: 1,604m *(5,262ft)*

Length: 24.5km *(15¼ miles)*

Average gradient: 6.6%

Maximum gradient: 20%

Vršič Pass & Mangart

With two Slovenians at the top of the sport, it seems only fair to offer two climbs in Slovenia that together make for one epic ascent.

Slovenia has recently come to the fore in professional cycling, with Primož Roglič and Tadej Pogačar battling it out for the biggest races in the world. Nestled between Italy, Austria, Hungary and Croatia, about half the size of Switzerland and with a population of just over two million, this state of the former Yugoslavia is not large. Yet Slovenia does cram in a lot of mountains and has the sort of roads that certainly inspire you to throw a leg over a top tube.

Arguably, the most spectacular climbs are nestled in the mountains in the northwest corner of the country. Yes, climbs plural. The Vršič Pass and Mangart go together like a saddle and seatpost, so here you're getting a two-for-one deal.

Starting in the ski town of Kranjska Gora, the Vršič Pass (road 206) has a gentle introduction. You wind across the Pišnica river a couple of times and the gradient is kind to cold muscles. The smell of pine is prevalent and it's all rather pleasant, which makes the arrival of the first hairpin after 2.5km (1½ miles) all the more surprising. Not only does the incline ramp up alarmingly as you approach the switchback, but cobbles also jolt you to attention. Then, as soon as you're round the bend, the vibrations disappear. They're back again as you approach the second hairpin less than 100m (109yd) later, but rough is always replaced with smooth as soon as the road straightens.

Each one of the 24 hairpins has cobbles. The surface is almost identical to the beautifully laid *pavé* of the St Gotthard Pass in Switzerland (see page 195), with the same fanned pattern to the stones. They certainly make you concentrate a little more, but these cobbles do not provide the same brutal experience as Flanders or Roubaix. Each hairpin is also numbered and the story goes that this is where the idea came from for numbering the hairpins on Alpe d'Huez.

If you're looking for a reason to give your legs a moment's rest, the perfect excuse comes just over halfway up the climb at hairpin number eight. Hidden in the trees is a beautiful little wooden Russian Orthodox chapel built in 1916, a year after the road was constructed. The pass became strategically important during the First World War because it led to the Isonzo Front and, to improve access, a road was built using Russian prisoners of war as labour. The Russians were also forced to clear the road of snow in winter, which led to the death of more than 100 prisoners and several guards during an avalanche in 1916. The chapel was built in memory of all those who died in both the avalanche and the construction of the road. In 2006, this side of the pass was also renamed The Russian Road.

From here to the summit at 1,611m (5,285ft) the gradient gets progressively harder, culminating in a final kilometre that averages 12%. The steepness you >>

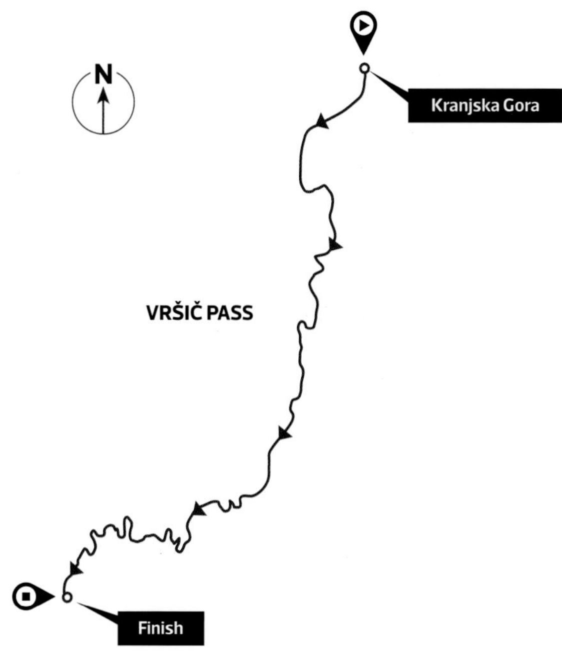

1600
1400
1200
1000
800m
0km
2
4
6
8
9.3

The Mangart is not a pass, just a road to a summit, but it's a dead end worth exploring

>> feel in your legs is matched by the steepness of the scenery, with a savagely saw-toothed skyline visible across the valley. These are the Julian Alps – named after Julius Caesar – with a beauty that is arguably a match for their near neighbours, the Dolomites.

For an even better look at the mountains, you need to continue over the summit of the Vršič Pass and descend to the base of the second climb. The Mangart is not a pass, simply a road to a summit, but it's a dead end worth exploring. It was built in 1938 by Italian troops, because this region of Slovenia was part of Italy at the time and had officially been so since the Treaty of Rapallo after the First World War (before that it was part of the Austro-Hungarian Empire).

You're now on a very narrow road and at times it feels as though it's barely clinging to the side of the mountains, but as it twists and turns through 13 hairpins and five tunnels it tests you even more than the Vršič, averaging more than 9% and hitting gradients of over 20%. As with the first climb, the Mangart begins in the trees, but when it reaches the altitude of the Vršič's summit the pines begin to melt away and the final 3km (1¾ miles) feels wonderfully exposed. The slim strip of tarmac teeters along under the peaks and above them all is the extraordinary dome-like mass of Mangart Mountain. It is Slovenia's fourth-highest peak at 2,679m (8,789ft), but its isolation makes it looks much more impressive than that figure suggests.

The last part of the climb swings round under huge cliff faces and there is plenty of evidence of rocks having fallen from above, which while unnerving will spur you on to the summit. Then, as you pedal out from under the cliffs, you'll find yourself at the junction of the one-way loop that takes you to the top. This is the highest road in Slovenia and the view >>

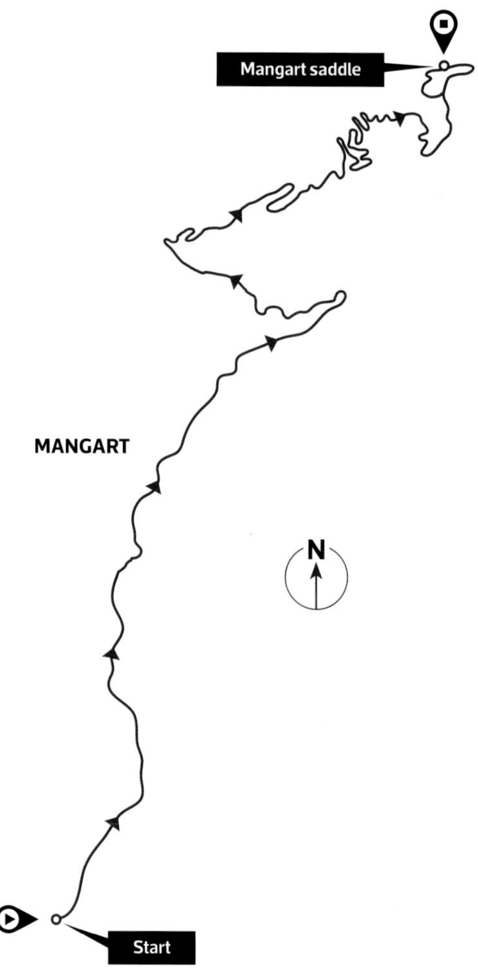

>> from the summit is certainly worth admiring before you begin the plummet back to the valley.

Talking of going downhill quickly, it's worth mentioning what lies just a few kilometres west of here. Perhaps it's because most pro cyclists don't have a life before cycling and therefore when one does it takes on an inflated fascination, but it seems impossible for commentators to talk about Roglič without slipping in the fact that he used to be a ski jumper. And cradled in these mountains is Planica, the home of Slovenian ski jumping and the highest ski jumping centre in the world. It was here that Roglič set his personal best jump of 185m (607ft) and it was also here on the Letalnica bratov Gorišek hill (the largest in the world) that he had a horrendous crash in 2007. Although he continued ski jumping for another four years, his progress stalled and he was overlooked for the Olympic Games so turned his attention to another sport. With roads like the Vršič Pass and Mangart on the doorstep of the ski centre, it's little wonder that that sport was cycling.

2000
1600
1200
800
400m
0km
4
8
12
16
20
24.5

Summit height: 705m *(2,313ft)*
Altitude gain: 652m *(2,139ft)*
Length: 7.9km *(5 miles)*
Average gradient: 8.2%
Maximum gradient: 10.2%

The Trollstigen

There's no guarantee you'll see trolls, but this Norwegian classic includes towering rock walls, waterfalls and truly spectacular views.

In photos, it looks familiar: a magnificent, serpentine road ascending through a work of art created entirely by nature. Rising from a verdant valley, the ribbon of tarmac snakes its way up into an ominously rugged landscape, surrounded by vast cliffs and jutting peaks dusted in snow. It looks for all the world like the Passo dello Stelvio (page 44), and it's an easy mistake to make given the tightly stacked hairpins on view, yet where the stats are concerned this climb is but David to the Stelvio's Goliath.

Located among the fjords of Norway, about 200km (124 miles) north of Bergen, the Trollstigen's actual summit stands at 858m (2,815ft), which is nearly two vertical kilometres lower than the Stelvio's. (Cyclists tackling the climb typically call it a day at a visitor centre approx. 150m/164yd below this peak.) It has only 11 hairpins to the Stelvio's 48, but just as in the biblical story, size and stature don't always mean supremacy. The sheer sense of wonder that greets riders on the Trollstigen far outweighs its vital statistics. >>

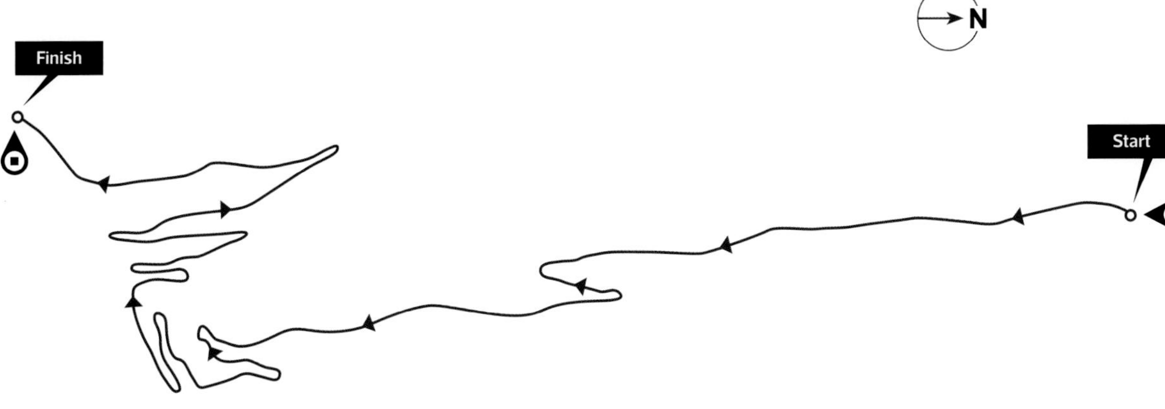

>> **One important thing to consider when planning a** trip here is the time of year. The Trollstigen is subject to winter closure but the actual dates vary each year – sometimes considerably – so you'll need to check in advance. To ride this incredible road, the best option is to head south from Åndalsnes. Glimpses of the distant peaks appear almost immediately as you leave the outskirts, serving as a teaser for what you will soon be getting up close and personal with. The contrast between the fjords and mountains here is striking and one of Norway's main attractions for cyclists.

A right turn after about 4km (2½ miles) takes you across the Rauma river and onto route 63, better known as the Troll Road in honour of the creatures that are a big part of Norwegian folklore. The mythical beings are often portrayed as spirits of the underground, with no certainty as to whether they are friend or foe to humans. Evidence suggests they were mostly feared, though, and so strongly did people believe in their existence that as recently as a few hundred years ago villages would ring the church bells to ward off these diminutive, grumpy souls. You'll encounter several trolls on the way up. Some are stone statues, some are wooden sculptures or images on signposts, but as for real ones? Well, you won't see them, but they may be watching you.

Some would have it that the turning onto the Troll Road is the start of the climb, but although the road does begin to rise for a time as it meanders through the lush Romsdalen valley, the tactically smart thing to do here is bide your time and save your legs. View this as a warm-up for the main act to follow and don't get excited prematurely, especially if you have any designs on troubling the sharp end of the Strava leaderboard.

A short descent returns you once more to the valley floor and a few more kilometres of false flat must still be covered before the true nature of this beast >>

You might think you're riding to a dead end, so vast and imposing is the wall of rock

>> reveals itself. Ahead lies an ascent of 7.9km (5 miles) up to the visitor centre, which most riders consider to be the summit of the 'main' Trollstigen climb. The shift in gradient as you begin the climb proper is noticeable but not too aggressive. The slope ramps up to a steady 6-7% and stays there for most of the climb. But be warned, the average is 8.2% thanks to a few steeper ramps in the mid-section nudging over 10%.

The first hairpin rolls around after about 2km (1¼ miles), and this is where things really start to get exciting. You're no longer cloistered by trees, so it's the first time you get to really appreciate the enormity of the landscape. Suddenly you feel rather small. However, it's approaching hairpin three when the true visceral impact of the Trollstigen really hits home.

At first glance, you might think you're riding to a dead end, so imposing and vast is the wall of rock ahead, but look closer and you'll see the road, a zigzag scar like Zorro's calling card in its sheer face. At this point, it's hard to keep your eyes on any one thing, let alone the road, so tempting is the scenery. Be sure to soak it in, because the Trollstigen packs a lot into a short distance. Particularly mesmerizing is the Stigfossen waterfall that cascades 320m (1,050ft) down the mountainside, passing directly under the road at about the halfway point in the climb.

Vertiginous cliff faces hang all around, but the 1,700-m (5,577-ft) Trollveggen, or the Troll Wall, that towers high above to the south is a main attraction. Its 1,000-m (3,281-ft) sheer face is the largest vertical drop in Europe and as such is a magnet for experienced climbers and, until it was banned, base jumpers. To the west are Bispen (1,450m/4,757ft), Kongen (1,614m/5,295ft) and Dronninga (1,701m/5,581ft); to the east Stigbottshornet (1,583m/5,194ft) and the Storgrovfjellet (1,629m/5,344ft).

Considering the hostility such a landscape presents to the passing of motor vehicles, it's hard to believe it took just eight years to construct the Trollstigen road, which opened in 1936. More recently, substantial government investment has ensured the road is impeccably maintained. There's no need for 30mm (1¼in) tyres and flexible seatposts here. Your derrière will be cosseted by a beautifully smooth strip of black tarmac the whole way up.

There's little by way of reprieve in the climb's upper reaches. The gradient hovers at around 7-8% but the reward is getting to enjoy a new perspective, having crossed to the opposite side of the valley. Those with a fear of heights might be less inclined to stare back down the climb, however, as there's not much by way of barriers. A row of rocks, each a few metres apart and resembling a troll's crooked teeth, is at times the only thing between you and the sheer drop.

And while we're on the subject of vertigo, once you finally reach the plateau and the visitor centre at around 700m (2,297ft), if your stomach allows, be sure to take the short stroll onto the viewing platform that juts out from the cliff edge, dangling some 200m (219yd) above the road below. It's a view you'll never forget.

The road might look familiar if you've ridden the Stelvio, but this is a climb with a beauty and a character all of its own.

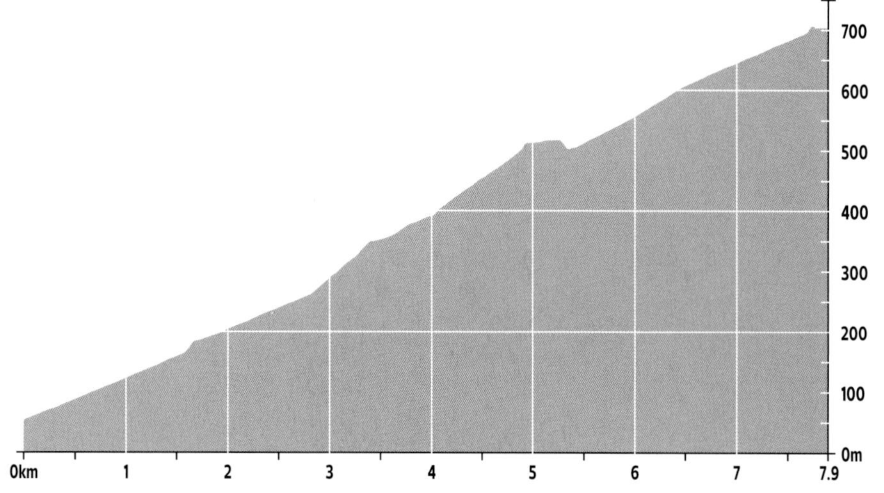

Summit height: 4,192m *(13,753ft)*
Altitude gain: 4,490m *(14,731ft)*
(factoring in undulations)
Length: 92km *(57 miles)*
Average gradient: 4.4%
Maximum gradient: 20%

Mauna Kea

This is it: the biggest, baddest climb of them all, rising an incredible 4,192m (13,753ft) over a distance of 92km (57 miles). Say *aloha* to our monster friend.

Imagine this: you're riding up the Col d'Izoard in the Alps. From Guillestre in the south it's a long slog of 31km (19 miles); the average gradient is reasonable at around 4%, but still you're thankful when you arrive at the summit. Except that when you get there you find yourself at the foot of Alpe d'Huez. Now you've got another 16km (10 miles) of climbing and the gradient has pitched up by quite a bit. Just as the summit of the Alpe arrives, you're transported to the base of the Col de la Croix de Fer and you have to face another 22km (14 miles) at 5%. And then it gets worse. After the Croix de Fer, you have to tackle the Mortirolo – 11km (7 miles) at 11% – followed immediately by Monte Zoncolan, a brutal ascent of 10km (6 miles) with an average gradient of 12% and spikes above 20%.

That, essentially, is what climbing Mauna Kea is like. Except it is potentially tougher as there's a 7.5-km (4¾-mile) section near the top that's loose gravel and has ramps of 20%, and the thin air at 4,000m (13,123ft) altitude means that every effort is amplified as your lungs fight to get enough oxygen. So serious is this climb that if you don't have a suitable 4x4 support vehicle, there's every chance that the local park rangers will simply refuse to let you continue to ride up the mountain.

Mauna Kea is a vast volcano on the largest of the Hawaiian Islands, commonly known as Big Island. Its summit is 4,207m (13,802ft) above sea level, but when measured from its base deep underwater it rises 10,211m (33,500ft), which when looked at in that sense makes it the tallest mountain in the world. Unlike the jagged peaks of the Alps or Himalayas, Mauna Kea is a great, rounded mass that squats benignly in the centre of the island, nuzzled up against its lower but more voluminous volcano sibling, Mauna Loa.

Its sheer size and position dominating everything around it means that, unsurprisingly, it was considered sacred by ancient Hawaiians, who believed it was the meeting point of the sky god Wakea and the land goddess Papa. Even today, native Hawaiian groups campaign to prevent development work, which they consider to be sacrilegious, taking place on Mauna Kea. The cause of their concern is a cluster of observatories at the summit, which have been built to take advantage of the clear skies and lack of light pollution, making this one of the world's foremost spots for stargazing.

Looking at Mauna Kea from the coast, it's hard to get a sense of the volcano's scale. Photographs don't do >>

>> it justice – the landscape is so broad and open that gradients don't seem to register. In truth, the only way to understand what the climb is like is to do it.

Begin by dipping a wheel in the sea. That way, you know that you are starting the ride from zero altitude, and the only way is up. The first section takes you from Waikoloa Beach, past the villas and hotels, and onto the Waikoloa Road. This is America, where the car is king, so the road is big, wide, long and most likely quite busy with traffic. Fortunately, the hard shoulder is also wide, affording plenty of space for cyclists to ride without fear of being crushed by Caddies and Chevvies.

Immediately the road tilts up, but at this point it is around 3% in gradient and it's only the strangely heavy feeling in your legs that lets you know you are gaining height. The palm trees of the coast give way to grass and scrubland pockmarked by patches of dark, volcanic rock, and the views go on endlessly into the distance.

The landscape is so featureless that it can be difficult to gauge distance, and by the time you arrive at the first major junction, a glance at your bike computer will reveal that you have ticked off 22km ($13\frac{2}{3}$ miles) and 765m (2,510ft) of ascent. A left turn is followed by a comparatively flat 7.5-km ($4\frac{2}{3}$-mile) section, before a right turn brings you onto the Old Saddle Road, so called because it sits in the curved valley between the two volcanoes. Again, the yellow line down the middle of the road seems to go on forever, but now the going is getting noticeably steeper and the surrounding countryside is getting greener, with patches of forest to offer an occasional defence from the wind. After 16km (10 miles) of uphill battle, the Old Saddle Road segues into the New Saddle Road, where the gradient relents slightly, but at 22km ($13\frac{2}{3}$ miles) would still be the main climb of any other ride.

By the time you arrive at the turnoff to the Mauna Kea Access Road, you will have already ridden uphill >>

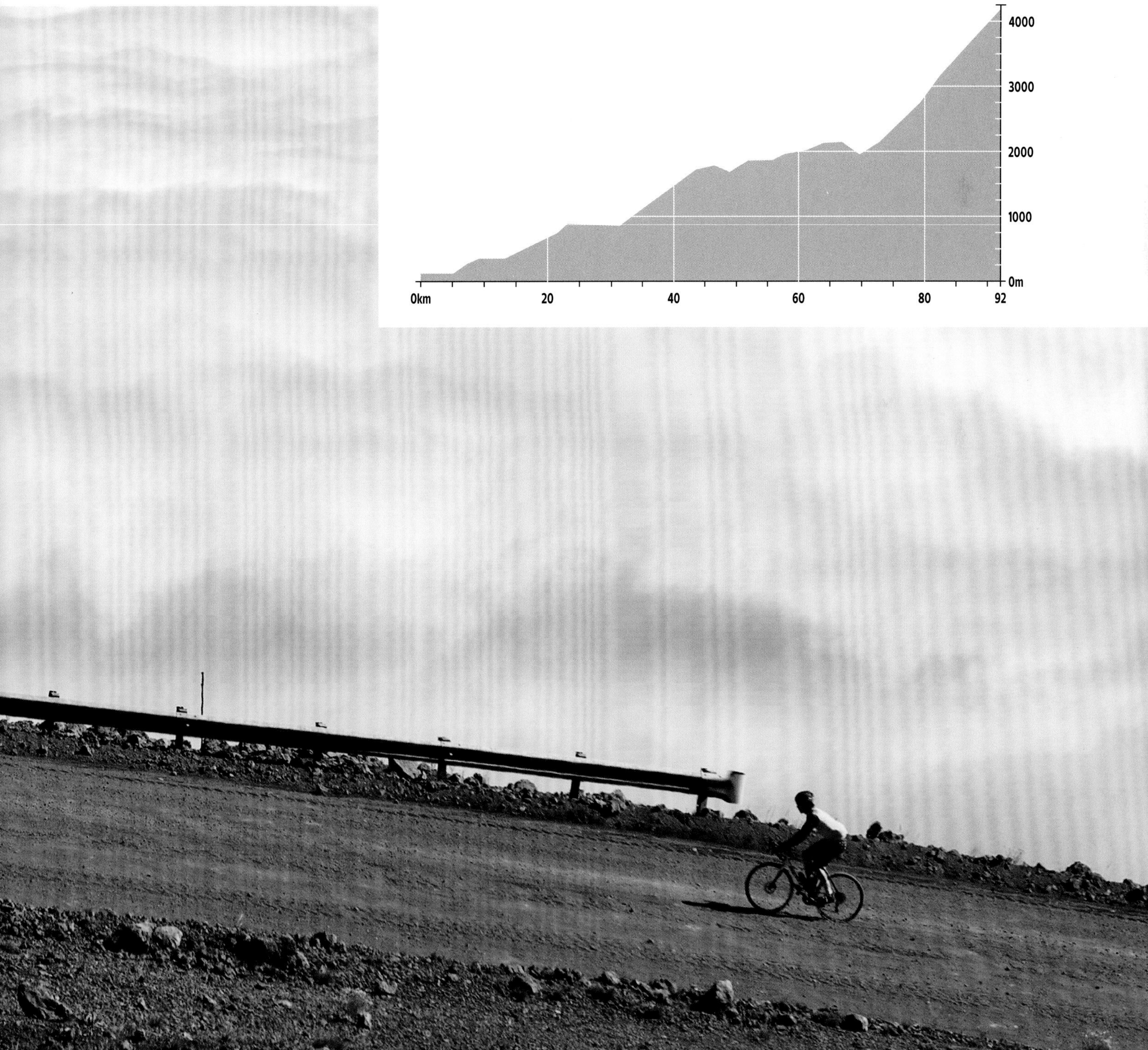

Only a tiny number of people can say they've conquered Mauna Kea

>> for 71km (44 miles) and gained more than 2,000m (6,562ft) of height (but done significantly more actual climbing than that, because the road is undulating). And the hard bit is just starting.

Almost unbelievably, there's still nearly 2,200m (7,218ft) of vertical ascent to come, averaging around 10% over 24km (15 miles) – the Zoncolan plus the Mortirolo. As if to mark the transition, the surrounding landscape becomes more dusty and barren as a sign that life at this altitude struggles to survive. The first 10km (6¼ miles) is on well-surfaced roads and includes nasty spikes of 15%. It comes to an end at the Visitor Centre, which is a great place to stop, eat, recover and realize that at 2,800m (9,186ft) you are now higher than any Alpine pass. You can also contemplate the sign that reads, 'Warning: hazardous road. Travel at your own risk beyond this point.'

It's here that many cyclists switch to a mountain bike, or at least change to wider gravel tyres and footwear better designed for walking – something you're almost guaranteed to be doing at some point soon. The next 7.5km (4⅔ miles) are on loose, slippery gravel with sections at 20%. Afterwards, the transition back to tarmac, while welcome, is just a reminder that there is still another steep, relentless 6-km (3¾-mile) climb to the summit.

To arrive at the observatories and look out over the moonscape above the clouds is to have completed one of the greatest challenges known to cycling. Only a tiny number of people can say they've conquered Mauna Kea, a climb that has a compelling claim to be the hardest in the world.

Pikes Peak

They say everything is bigger in America, and Pikes Peak in Colorado towers over anything that Europe has to offer.

The American passion for the motor car is reflected in the country's roads. Even when the landscape is wild, the altitude suffocating and the destination a dead end, the road will be wide, smooth and inviting. There are no half measures here. Once it has been decided that a gravel track is no longer sufficient, it will be replaced by a thoroughfare that can be cruised in comfort by Cadillacs, SUVs, Chevrolets, and motorhomes wider than some houses. Forget about the narrow tarmac strip so often found snaking up the side of mountains in Europe – in the United States, even above an altitude of 4,000m (13,123ft), you'll find a road where two buses could pass each other on a corner without fear of touching wing mirrors.

So it is with Pikes Peak in Colorado. The broad road to its summit gives the impression of a state highway, with its double yellow line meandering upwards like the gentle curves of a slow-moving river. It would be easy to assume, therefore, that the climb is equally benign for cyclists – just a case of ticking off the kilometres in the unhurried fashion of a day-trip in an open-top Chevvy. That assumption would be a mistake.

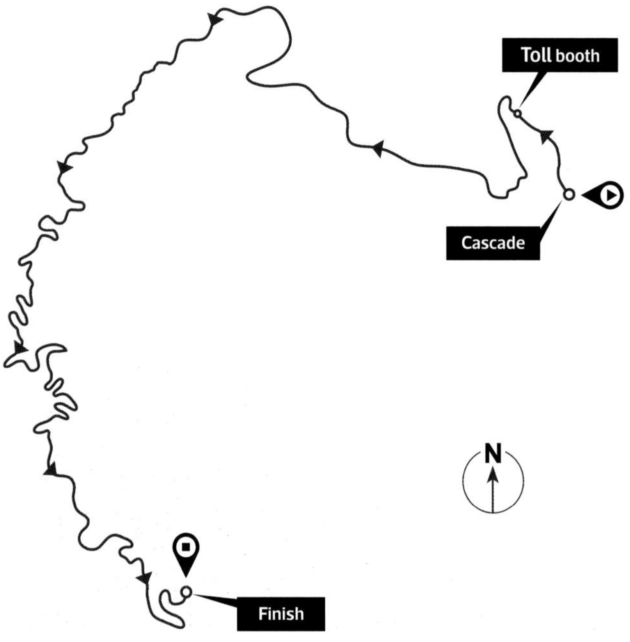

Toll booth

Cascade

Finish

N

Any misconceptions about the severity of Pikes Peak soon evaporate on an analysis of the stats. This is the second-highest paved road in the United States, just a few metres short of neighbouring Mount Evans (but with more continuous ascent). Before you even start the climb you are at an altitude – 2,190m (7,185ft) – similar to the summits of many of the big passes in the Alps. Above this height is where altitude sickness starts to kick in, and there is still another 2,112m (6,929ft) of vertical ascent to go until the summit of Pikes Peak. Climbing it is essentially like starting from the top of Alpe d'Huez and then heading upwards to do the elevation of Alpe d'Huez twice over again.

Then there's the gradient. The average of 6.6% over 31km (19¼ miles) may seem fairly amenable, however that figure is skewed by a few flattish sections and even a stretch of downhill. Take a closer look at the profile and you'll spot an 11-km (6¾-mile) section at about midway – kilometres 14–25 (miles 9–16) – where the gradient rarely dips below 10%. Those big, wide roads make it hard to gauge just how steep this climb is.

If the thin air and severe gradient don't get you, there are always the bears. And the mountain lions. And the rattlesnakes. Or, if you're really unlucky, you could find yourself in the path of a car trying to break the record for the fastest ascent of Pikes Peak. That milestone has belonged to some famous names in motor racing, with the record being broken in 2013 by nine-time World Rally Champion Sébastien Loeb before factory Porsche racing driver Romain Dumas became the first driver to dip below eight minutes in 2018, at an average speed >>

Summit height: 4,302m *(14,114ft)*
Altitude gain: 2,112m *(6,929ft)*
Length: 31km *(19¼ miles)*
Average gradient: 6.6%
Maximum gradient: 13%

If the thin air and gradient don't get you, there are always the bears

>> of nearly 150km/h (93mph). That's pretty impressive for a route that includes 156 bends.

Fortunately, those records were set during the annual Pikes Peak International Hill Climb, a race that began in 1916 when the road was little more than a gravel trail. The race is traditionally held in June, so check that your dates don't clash if you're planning a two-wheeled ascent. Then you're ready to go.

Slap bang in the middle of Colorado is the city of Colorado Springs. A few kilometres west is Manitou Springs, a good base for tackling Pikes Peak. About 10km (6¼ miles) further along Highway 24 is the small town of Cascade, where a turning off the highway marks the start of the climb. After a couple of kilometres, you arrive at the wooden toll booths that guard the entrance to the mountain road, but being on bikes you glide past the queue of cars and wave merrily to the attendants as you ride through the barrier – only for them to run out and shout at you to stop.

Yes, cyclists have to pay an entrance fee, too. It's also worth checking ahead to make sure the road is open. Officially it is open all year, but changeable conditions mean it can be closed if the weather is bad.

Once you've paid your entrance fee, the road winds upwards through dense forests of pine and junipers >>

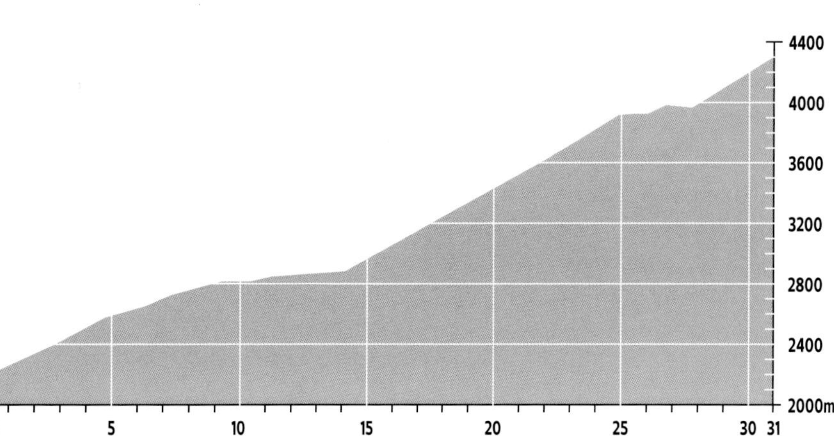

>> that block the view but shield the wary cyclist from the enormity of the task ahead. Here, you're in the 'Foothills Zone', an area up to around 2,500m (8,202ft) elevation where the flora is luscious and plentiful.

After 9km (5½ miles), there's a moment of respite when the road dips and then flattens out along the edge of Crystal Creek Reservoir, before continuing its relentless ascent into the 'Montane Zone', where the trees become stubbier and more sparse as the air gets thinner. Here, the rocky domes of the summit appear in the distance, and the road starts to twist and turn as the gradient creeps up into double figures.

Above 3,000m (9,842ft), you enter the 'Sub-Alpine Zone', where only the hardiest trees and shrubs survive in an increasingly barren rocky landscape. This ends at the Glen Cove Inn, where it's sensible to stop and refuel. After 20km (12½ miles) and 1,200m (3,937ft) of climbing, the hard part is just about to begin.

Beyond Glen Cove is the 'Alpine Zone', where the lack of oxygen and the harsh weather conditions make it almost impossible for anything to survive. As such, the final 10km (6¼ miles) and 800m (2,625ft) of climbing is through a desolate moonscape of brown rock, punctuated only by the occasional patch of green moss.

By the top, even in the height of summer, snow covers the bare dome of rubble, and a squat building (thankfully housing a cafe) provides the only shelter from the biting wind. The air is so thin it's not a place to linger for too long – just long enough to grab a coffee and contemplate the achievement of conquering a climb that dwarfs those of its European cousins.

The views from the summit over Colorado and the Rocky Mountains stretch on forever, but perhaps the most wonderful sight of all is the swooping, sinuous descent to come – all 31km (19¼ miles) of it on that wide, smooth, all-American road.

Index

Page numbers in *italics* refer to illustrations, charts and maps

---

Writing credits (page numbers refer to the first page of the ride):

Introduction Michael Donlevy; 204 Stu Bowers; 10, 16, 20, 26, 32, 38, 44, 50, 64, 90, 94, 100, 108, 114, 120, 126, 132, 138, 144, 150, 156, 160, 166, 172, 178, 184, 192, 198 Henry Catchpole; 56, 76, 82, 210, 216 Pete Muir; 70 James Spender

Photography credits (page numbers refer to the first page of the ride):

70 Juan Trujillo Andrades; 198, 204 Paul Calver; 82 James Cannon; 10, 16, 20, 26, 32, 38, 44, 50, 64, 90, 94, 100, 108, 114, 120, 126, 132, 138, 144, 150, 156, 160, 166, 172, 178, 184 Alex Duffill; 56, 76, 192, 210 Patrik Lundin; 216 Geoff Waugh

First published in Great Britain in 2022 by Mitchell Beazley, an imprint of
Octopus Publishing Group Ltd, Carmelite House
50 Victoria Embankment, London EC4Y 0DZ
www.octopusbooks.co.uk
www.octopusbooksusa.com

An Hachette UK Company
www.hachette.co.uk

Distributed in the US by Hachette Book Group
1290 Avenue of the Americas, 4th and 5th Floors, New York, NY 10104

Distributed in Canada by Canadian Manda Group
664 Annette St. Toronto, Ontario, Canada M6S 2C8

ISBN 978-1-78472-809-0

A CIP catalogue record for this book is available from the British Library.

Printed and bound in China

10 8 6 4 2 1 3 5 7 9

Disclaimer: All routes were open at the time of going to press,
but please check for road closures before setting out on a ride.

Text compiled by Michael Donlevy
Editorial Director: Joe Cottington
Art Director: Juliette Norsworthy
Designer: Geoff Fennell
Senior Editor: Faye Robson
Senior Production Manager: Katherine Hockley